Shock Theatre
Chicago Style

*WBKB-TV's Late Night
Horror Showcase, 1957–1959*

Donald F. Glut

Foreword by Kerry Bennett

Afterword by Dick Dyszel,
"Count Gore De Vol"

McFarland & Company, Inc., Publishers
Jefferson, North Carolina, and London

OTHER DONALD F. GLUT WORKS FROM MCFARLAND
(CHRONOLOGICALLY): *The Frankenstein Catalog, Being a Comprehensive Listing of ...* [all media] (1984), *Dinosaurs: The Encyclopedia* (1997; there are seven very substantial supplements, each with the title *Dinosaurs: The Encyclopedia, Supplement 1* [etc.]: 2000, 2002, 2003, 2006, 2008, 2010, 2012), *Dinosaur Valley Girls: The Book* (1998), *Carbon Dates: A Day by Day Almanac of Paleo Anniversaries and Dino Events* (1999), *Jurassic Classics: A Collection of Saurian Essays and Mesozoic Musings* (2001), *The Frankenstein Archive: Essays on the Monster, the Myth, the Movies, and More* (2002), *I Was a Teenage Movie Maker: The Book* (2007)

Frontispiece: Classic portrait of Terry Bennett as Marvin, the horror host of Chicago television's *Shock Theatre.*

LIBRARY OF CONGRESS CATALOGUING-IN-PUBLICATION DATA

Glut, Donald F.
    Shock theatre Chicago style : WBKB-TV's late night horror showcase, 1957–1959 / Donald F. Glut ; foreword by Kerry Bennett ; afterword by Dick Dyszel, "Count Gore De Vol."
        p.   cm.
    Includes bibliographical references and index.

    ISBN 978-0-7864-6805-8
    softcover : acid free paper ∞

    1. Shock theater (Television program : Chicago, Ill.)
2. Bennett, Terry, 1930–1977.   3. Television personalities —
Illinois — Chicago — Biography.   4. Television programs —
Illinois — Chicago — History.   I. Title.
PN1992.77.S525G58 2012
791.45'72 — dc23   2012024867

BRITISH LIBRARY CATALOGUING DATA ARE AVAILABLE

On the cover: Terry Bennett (right) as *Shock Theatre* host "Mad" Marvin, surrounded by some of the characters that appeared with him on the show (photograph courtesy Kerry Bennett)

Front cover design by Mark Berry (www.hot-cherry.co.uk).

Manufactured in the United States of America

McFarland & Company, Inc., Publishers
  Box 611, Jefferson, North Carolina 28640
    www.mcfarlandpub.com

In fondest memory of
Terry and Joy Bennett
("Marvin" and "Dear").
You were the best!

Table of Contents

Acknowledgments

The author thanks sincerely the following people who contributed in some way, either directly or indirectly, to my writing this book:

Lyle Conway, for sharing so much imagery and so many personal memories of *Shock Theatre* as well as other local Chicago television programs; Ted Okuda and Mark Yurkiw, authors of the book *Chicago TV Horror Movie Shows: From Shock Theatre to Svengooli*, a treasury of information, including interviews with some of the people who made such shows happen in the Windy City; William Sumner, art librarian, Chicago Public Library, for researching the air dates of many of the movies shown on *Shock Theatre*; Rick Thomas (AKA "Lazlo, Keeper of the Dead" of *Graveyard Theatre*), for sharing with me photographs from *Shock Theatre,* his interviews with Joy Bennett and Bruce Newton, and conversations with Marjorie Harris; Terry Tiz, president of the "Dead-Beats Fan Club," who supplied me with audio recordings of *Shock Theatre* and *Shocktail Party*, photos, even sheet music, plus much information regarding the Deadbeats and those shows; and Margaret "Maggie" Walters, former secretary of "The Only Official Terry Bennett Fan Club" (and a high school classmate) for remembering so much about *Shock Theatre* and its people.

Many thanks to Ronny Born, who played "Orville" on *Shock Theatre,* and the late Bruce Newton, who played "Shorty" (AKA "Frankie") on *Shock Theatre* and either furnished or created many of the props for the shows, and Marjorie Harris, former secretary for WBKB and *Shock Theatre.*

Also thanks to Phil Anselmini; Natasha Beals, membership representative, American Federation of Television and Recording Artists/Screen Actors Guild (AFTRA/SAG), Chicago; Bob Burns, of *Jeepers Creepers Theater* in Los Angeles and another *Shock Theater* in San Antonio, Texas; Larry M. Byrd; George Chastain; creator of the website "E-Gore's Chamber of TV Horror Hosts" (www.horrorhosts.com); Sandy Clark, John H. Hudgens and Michael Monahan, producers of the *American Scary* DVD (www.americanscary.com);

Left to right: The author, in 1958, with Terry Bennett and Marvin fans Dan McCarthy and Joe Kampf outside the Bennetts' Ashland Avenue apartment. Photographer: Victor Fabian.

Bill Cunningham; Kent Daluga; Allen A. Debus; Dennis Druktenis, publisher and editor of *Scary Monsters* magazine; Dick Dyszel (AKA "Count Gore De Vol" of the long- and still-running *Creature Feature*); the late Bill Feret, "Shock Absorber" *numero uno* and former president of "The Only Official Terry Bennett Fan Club"; Dan Golden; Richard Hagopian; Jan Alan Henderson; Roger Hill; Eric L. Hoffman; Brett Hominick; Bob Isaacson; Roy G. Kempa; Dennis and Judy Kessler; Kurt Kuersteiner (www. radiohorrorhosts.com); James Lee; Daniel H. McCarthy and Claudia McCarthy; Daniel J. Mullen; Ted Newsom; Fred Olen Ray; Martin Riccardo; the late Joe Sarno; the late Mark Shepard, former president of the Ghoulita Fan Club; Mike Stein, publisher and editor of *Filmfax* magazine; Brinke Stevens; Sid Terror, for information regarding Maila Nurmi (AKA "Vampira"); John Skerchock; Roy Thomas; Harvey Tow; Bill Warren, author of the book *Keep Watching the Skies! The 21st Century Edition*; and Deborah Webb.

A very special thanks to the late Joy "Dear" Bennett and to her son Kerry Bennett for sharing with me so many photographs, newspaper and magazine print material, original scripts, personal memories and whatever else they could find or remember regarding "good ol' Shockaroo Theatre" and the one and only Terry ("Marvin") Bennett.

And, of course, to the late (and great) Terry Bennett, who not only created and portrayed Marvin on Chicago's *Shock Theatre*, but also spared some of his valuable time one afternoon to put up with a group of pesky teenage fans who showed up at his door unannounced one very memorable sunny day in 1958.

I apologize to anyone else deserving thanks that I may have inadvertently missed.

Foreword by Kerry Bennett

As long as I can remember, I've always had a fascination with my father's show biz past. And growing up in Tampa, Florida, in the early 1970s, I witnessed a fair share of his abilities. There were a few brief stints on television, a radio show or two, even a job as a news anchor. But I was assured by my mom, years after his death, that "it wasn't like the old days."

Unfortunately, I never had the opportunity to "pick his brain" or listen to countless hours of stories about the golden age of live TV. I was only ten years old when he passed away, yet there were still remnants of those years gone by. As a child, I remembered seeing old boxes stored in our garage filled with various puppets and half-completed dummies made of *papier mâché*. There were dozens of old typewritten stories and characters developed for some future project that never materialized, photos and newspaper clippings from his early days as a teenage ventriloquist (or "vent," as professionals seem to prefer calling themselves) touring the country, props and handwritten storyboards from his work in children's television.

But there was one aspect of his past that fascinated me the most.

In our garage, stored high above in the rafters, was a 16 × 20" portrait of my father as Marvin, host of Chicago's *Shock Theatre*. Kids in the neighborhood used to dare each other to peek through the side window of our garage to view the painting. It didn't help matters that my brother's spray-painted name on the interior garage wall, Kip, was misinterpreted by many as "R.I.P."

My mother did her best to make sure that our father's work was never forgotten. There were stories of "big crowds," "celebrity friends," "high ratings." And while I never entirely doubted my mother's accounts of the past, there was a certain degree of skepticism. But I was spellbound by what little I knew about *Shock Theatre* and wanted to know more. I yearned for a non-biased account of the show, separating truth from the myth.

Ten years ago, with a new sense of discovery and drive, I was inspired to look through those old dilapidated boxes that were still in storage at my mother's house, boxes that I hadn't seen since we moved to Florida in 1972. By this time, most of the boxes were gone, the contents either discarded or disintegrated over time, but several still remained. I pored through what seemed like an endless collection of newspaper clippings, magazine pages, black-and-white photos and, much to my surprise, dozens of original *Shock Theatre* scripts. In addition there was that portrait of Marvin that I remember as a kid, even the "magnifying" eyeglasses that Marvin wore.

With the advent of the Internet, a new range of possibilities awaited me and my "true" search began in earnest. Through various searches and email exchanges, I was encouraged to contact Don Glut immediately. There was a degree of urgency in the request. It turns out that Don didn't just remember the show, he had intimate knowledge of nearly every aspect of Chicago's *Shock Theatre*. Between years of email correspondence, "trading notes" and sharing his knowledge, I've learned more than I could have ever imagined. Through his deluge of memories and insight, memorabilia and, above all, friendship, Don has allowed me a glimpse into a world that meant so much to him, and to so many others. I can think of no one more qualified to write about Chicago's *Shock Theatre*.

Thank you, Don. I found what I was searching for.

St. Petersburg, Florida • 2012

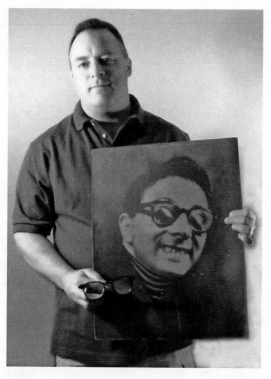

Kerry Bennett holding the original glasses worn by his father Terry Bennett as Marvin on *Shock Theatre* and the portrait of Marvin used as a prop on the show (courtesy Kerry Bennett).

Introduction

My favorite local Chicago television program was — and always will be — *Shock Theatre.*

When the show premiered at 10:00 PM on Saturday, December 7, 1957, on local ABC television affiliate WBKB-TV (now WLS-TV, still Channel 7), I — then 13 years old and in the seventh grade at St. Andrew Grammar School — was in for a surprise.

I'd been prepared for the station premiering *Frankenstein*, the original movie starring my then (and still) favorite actor Boris Karloff. But that was about all I knew about what was to transpire on our home TV set that night.

By December 1957, I had already seen, in neighborhood theatres as Realart reissues, most of the Universal Frankenstein movies, indeed, all of them — including *Abbott and Costello Meet Frankenstein—except* for the three starring Karloff (*Frankenstein, Bride of Frankenstein* and *Son of Frankenstein*). I'd heard that Karloff's portrayal of the Monster was the best; I'd loved the other Frankenstein movies I had already seen, and was particularly anxious to see the movie that had begun the series.

Frankenstein, with the usual commercial interruptions, was *all* that I expected to see that Saturday night.

I was in for a pleasant ... shock.

On Sunday, December 1, after getting hold of our family newspaper the *Chicago Sun-Times*, I anxiously yanked out that week's *TV Prevue*, the paper's small and free *TV Guide*–like booklet. I knew that finding a photo of Boris Karloff on the cover as Frankenstein's Monster was way too much to hope for (what was featured was a color picture of actors Ward Bond and Robert Horton from *Wagon Train*). Hastily flipping the pages to check out the Saturday night shows, I stopped at page 47, where I read the listing for 10 o'clock:

PREMIERE. Shock Theater.......7
"Frankenstein." See index.

The index summed up the plot of *Frankenstein* perhaps too simply: "Scientist creates artificial life, only to have his monster run amuck [*sic*]. Boris Karloff, Colin Clive (1932)." That single sentence offered some idea as to what *Frankenstein* was about; but what was this "*Shock Theater*" (usually and officially spelled *Theatre*) so casually mentioned in *TV Prevue*?

For the answer I'd have to wait one *very long* week (not unlike, in early June, that final week of school before it shut it doors for summer vacation). At the week's end there was the *even longer* (or so it seemed) Saturday night leading up to the Chicago TV debuts of both *Frankenstein* and that mysterious "*Shock Theater.*"

Our family usually ate dinner at 5:00, after which we all sat down in the living room to watch our favorite evening television shows.

On that particular Saturday, starting at 6:00 PM, we went through the usual batch of programs: *Boston Blackie* (Blackie solves the murder of a police detective's brother), followed by *Perry Mason* ("The Case of the Neglected Nymph," an episode wherein Perry defends a girl caught burglarizing her former employer's home), *Topper* ("House Wreckers," with Cosmo's house needing to be moved to make way for a new freeway), *The Gale Storm Show* (Susanna and Nugey anticipating attending the New Orleans Mardi Gras), *Have Gun, Will Travel* (Paladin accompanies an Englishman to his newly inherited Montana ranch), *Gunsmoke* (Matt Dillon confronts a dirt farmer accused of neglecting his destitute family) and, finally, *Hit Parade* (current songs performed by Jill Corey, Virginia Gibson, Tommy Leonetti and my future friend Alan Copeland).

Ordinarily I would have enjoyed all of those programs as much as the rest of my family did. But on that seventh of December, the shows seemed to drag on forever.

Eventually 10 o'clock did arrive.

For the record, the competition that night included *Dr. Hudson's Secret Journal* ("Dream Cottage"), a show we usually did watch — that is, until *Shock Theatre* occupied the same timeslot; and the 1940s movies *The Postman Always Rings Twice* and *Boomerang*. I settled back on the living room couch with a big bowl of buttered popcorn, prepared by my Mom using the old shaking-pot method, and a large bottle of Coca-Cola, and switched the TV channel knob to the seven position.

Shock Theatre began with crashing lightning followed by what looked like a haunted house, these visuals accompanied by mysterious music, spooky sound effects and a woman's screams ... and finally by the appearance of a weird but also handsome and cool-looking character who, speaking in a rather mellow tenor voice not unlike that of actor Peter Lorre, introduced himself as Marvin. The show's genial host, he was dressed like a beatnik — all in black, his garb including a turtleneck sweater and sport jacket. And he wore a pair of horn-rimmed glasses with impossibly thick lenses that magnified his eyes to several times their natural size.

Marvin (played by someone I'd soon learn was a veteran ventriloquist named Terry Bennett) wasn't *just* a beatnik; he was totally mad, a horror-crazed fiend who, while sometimes cackling insanely, got supreme delight from murdering, maiming and/or dismembering the other character introduced on *Shock Theatre*'s opening night: a sexy young woman whose face was not seen, referred to originally as simply "Dear" (or, on occasion, "Her" or even "She").

This Marvin guy was like a long-lost, forgotten or hidden-away relative of Lorre, albeit one who had read and absorbed, in addition to the more horrific writings of Poe, the works of Ginsberg and Kerouac, thus becoming the most ghoulish member of the Beat Generation. And yet, despite the often horrendous acts we would watch Marvin perform that night (and in the weeks to come), the character was tremendously appealing, even endearing. He could make us shudder, that was true; but more often, with his distinct brand of gallows humor, he made us laugh.

By 11:30 *Frankenstein* ended, and *Shock Theatre* and its mad beatnik host were gone — at least for this week. Following *Shock Theatre* on WBKB was *Wrestling*.

Not a wrestling fan, I chose to follow my first jolt of *Shock* with a rerun of *Inner Sanctum*, a TV offshoot of a popular long-running radio series that, in its original audio incarnation at least, had its own "horror host" (as such characters would be called in later years). That night's *Inner Sanctum* mystery was entitled "Guilty Secret," about a young man who suspects that his mother murdered his stepfather, who had been a famous actor. But the comparatively minor chills that program offered could compete in no way with those I'd just experienced watching *Frankenstein* ... and also Marvin.

By the time Marvin had uttered his closing words on that debut telecast, I — like so many viewers that night, presumably mostly teenagers — was completely hooked on the character and his show. Almost instantly, to me and so many other fans, Marvin had taken on the status of a rock 'n' roll, sports or movie star. More than that, as one Saturday night would follow the next, he'd become a kind of sinister yet lovable honorary big brother.

Although I was no beatnik, I soon found myself dressing like Marvin, all in black and with that trademark turtleneck sweater, wardrobe choices I would maintain for decades. And while I no longer (or, at least, not that often) lapse into mimicking Marvin's lines or his distinctive fiendish laugh, I do — to this day — more than occasionally dress in black.

How surprised and delighted I was when, one day in early 1958, my teenage friend and neighbor Daniel H. (Danny) McCarthy told me that his father, also named Dan, worked at WBKB-TV and handled security for *Shock Theatre*!

I pestered Danny a lot to get me onto the *Shock Theatre* set; alas, that dream was never realized. Danny never visited the set either, although his dad did take his younger sister Claudia to the WBKB studio to see the show being performed before the live TV cameras. "I couldn't believe how small [the set] was," Claudia McCarthy recently emailed her brother. "A tiny corner of the studio. Who knew?" Danny did, however, via his dad, get me a photograph of Marvin that Terry Bennett autographed on the reverse side.

Although I never was fortunate actually to set foot on the *Shock Theatre* set, I did — just once — get to meet both Terry Bennett and his beautiful wife Joy who, at the time, was enacting the role of "Dear" on the program. Someone, possibly Danny or my friend Victor Fabian, the latter as big a fan of *Shock Theatre* as I, discovered that Terry Bennett was listed in the Chicago telephone directory. Upon hearing this, I immediately rushed to our White Pages and thumbed through the "Bs." Sure enough, there was a listing for "Bennett, Terry." The directory also gave *this* Terry Bennett's street address.

Could this possibly be *the* Mr. Bennett? This Terry Bennett lived on Ashland Avenue, not far from my house and north of Lake View High School (which another ventriloquist, the legendary Edgar Bergen, had long ago attended).

Surely finding out if this was *our* Terry Bennett was worth a trip down to the Ashland address. And so, a day or so later, Danny, Victor, another friend named Joe Kampf and I found ourselves huddled outside an Ashland Avenue apartment building trying to work up sufficient nerve to press the Bennetts' buzzer. The sun was shining and the weather was pleasant, so atypical for a day to meet the murderous madman from *Shock Theatre*.

We checked the name on the hallway door buzzer and confirmed that name, "Terry Bennett." As to pressing the buzzer, all of us chickened out and hurried back outside, waiting again until Vic proclaimed that he would do the honors.

Vic disappeared back into the hallway as Danny, Joe and I walked back to the sidewalk. Then we waited — forever, it seemed, with no idea what might happen next. Was Vic a captive in the apartment dungeon of Mad Marvin, as the character was sometimes called; or were the Bennetts holding him until the police arrived to haul off to "juvie hall" and then reform school these four teenaged trespassers?

Finally the front door opened and out stepped Victor accompanied by —

The author (with glasses) *as* Marvin at his fourteenth "Shocktail" birthday party in February, 1958. Fellow "Shock Absorbers," from left to right: (top row) Joe Kampf, Bert Ott, Jim Neveau, (bottom row) Bob Genovaldi, Paul Klug, Ray Genovaldi and Gene Gronemeyer.

yes, wearing horn-rimmed glasses, although not the magnifying specs used on the show — the real and authentic *Terry (Marvin) Bennett!*

That experience and so many of its details will forever remain among my fondest memories (see picture, page x).

Terry, in no way peeved that we'd barged into his privacy and brought our fanaticism for his character and show to his very doorstep, graciously posed for photos, signed autographs and answered our "fannish" questions. When I asked Terry if I could get a picture of him *strangling* me, as he so often did his wife on the show, he happily obliged. Tragically, while I survived the assault, when Vic snapped my camera's shutter his hand moved slightly, forever blurring the moment. At least my memory of the event remains in sharp focus.

Of one thing we were all certain. Clearly Terry enjoyed meeting his fans, even such pushy and intrusive ones as we four.

We briefly met the beautiful Joy Bennett that eventful day, too; but in keeping with the gag of the program, I snapped her photo only from behind.

At least twice — by proxy, anyway — I actually got to *be* Marvin.

For my fourteenth birthday, in February of 1958, my Mother threw me a party. One of my friends suggested that I make the event a "shocktail party," a term often spoken by Marvin on his show. Agreeing that the idea was a good one, I put on my black turtleneck and sport coat, donned a large pair of thick-rimmed glasses and greeted my guests as Marvin would have, imitating his trademark greeting, "H'lo! I'm Marvin," accompanied by a quick wave.

At the time, live "spook shows" or "ghost shows" were still popular events held in Chicago theatres. Most popular during the 1940s and 1950s, "spook shows," the most famous being *Dr. Silkini's Asylum of Horrors*, were live stage presentations usually hosted by a professional magician. Most of the show comprised a series of magic acts, often with a supernatural theme (*e.g.*, materializing the "ghost" of the recently late James Dean), with some audience participation. Such shows usually climaxed with various familiar monsters — the most popular being Frankenstein's — appearing on stage, then, as the house lights were gradually doused, stalking menacingly into the audience. Following this blackout, the house lights would come back on, after which the audience would see a horror movie, too often it seemed *The Bowery Boys Meet the Monsters*.

I decided to put on such a show in our basement, again in the guise and persona of Marvin, following the show with some amateur monster movies I had made, plus whatever cut-down Castle Films editions of Universal horror films I owned at the time.

Naturally I became a loyal and dedicated member of "The Only Official Terry Bennett Fan Club," run by a teenager, a little older than I, named Bill Feret, arguably Marvin Fan (or "Shock Absorber") Number One. Marvin frequently cited Bill on the show, read his poems and jokes, and eventually plugged the fan club.

One day in 1959 I decided to track down Bill Feret. Discovering that Bill lived on Leavitt Street, not far from my family's house, I visited him, paid the required dues, received my membership card and copy of the club's "FIRST JOURNAL — SUMMER — 1959," and became an official member.

In 1960, the year following *Shock Theatre*'s cancellation, a letter I'd written to the fan club was very belatedly answered by the fan club's secretary Margaret (or Maggie) Walters. Included with her letter were two photos of Terry and Joy. Coincidentally Maggie would, in 1960, become a fellow junior-level classmate of mine at St. Benedict High School.

From that point on I lost contact with both Bill and the fan club — for a long time, anyway.

Decades later I was commissioned by the American Museum of Natural

History in New York City to give a lecture on the history of dinosaur movies in their main auditorium. On a lark, the night before the lecture and with some free time to fill, I checked the telephone book for the name of John Zacherle—a TV "horror host" who predated Marvin on his own *Shock Theatre*—and, as with Terry Bennett years before, found "Zach" and his home number listed. I invited "Zach" to be a guest at my presentation and, to my delight, he showed up.

Ironically, Marvin fan club president Bill Feret, now a long-time New York resident and a successful author, was also present for that same talk. Although Bill only had a vague memory of me visiting his upstairs flat in Chicago, and didn't remember at all until I reminded him of that day, he said he did keep in touch with Terry and Joy for a while after they moved to the East Coast. It was on that night that Bill told me the sad news that Terry had passed away.

My memories of *Shock Theatre* and the Bennetts remained strong and warm.

In early 2002 I received an email from Kerry Bennett, who, to my surprise, included the local Chicago call letters WBKB in his email address. Kerry explained that he was Terry and Joy's son and that he was interested in a TV show that his parents had done called *Shock Theatre*. Kerry's email was in response to a letter I had written about the show that was published in a recent issue of *Filmfax*, a magazine devoted to old movies, TV shows, their personnel and also to other forms of popular entertainment. There were some errors concerning his dad in my letter, misinformation based mostly on gossip, and Kerry wanted to set the record straight.

Soon my friends Lyle Conway and Rick Thomas also began corresponding with Kerry. Lyle, a sculptor and special effects artist for *The Dark Crystal*, *Clash of the Titans*, *The Little Shop of Horrors*, and many other motion pictures, also had fond memories of *Shock Theatre*.

Although Rick was too young to have actually seen the show, he was truly fascinated by it as well as the horror host concept, patterning his own "Lazlo, Keeper of the Dead" character and *Graveyard Theatre* cable TV show on what he could find out about *Shock Theatre*. Rick became *so* immersed in researching Chicago's *Shock Theatre* that he originally planned to write a book about the show, a project that would eventually morph into an article with interviews with Joy Bennett and show alumnus Bruce Newton, published in *Filmfax* #104 (October–December 2004).

Around that time I was also able to track down Maggie Walters, now living in Texas, and pick her brain for more memories of *Shock Theatre*.

Kerry's original email opened up a continuing friendship that included, in the too-brief years before her passing, his mother Joy. I shared my own recollections of the show and his parents with Kerry, answering as many of his questions as I could. Our emails also gave me the opportunity to have Joy—through Kerry—answer a number of my own questions about *Shock Theatre*. And of course I sent the Bennetts copies of the pictures my friends and I had snapped that wonderful afternoon outside Terry and Joy's Ashland Avenue apartment building.

Eventually I received a couple hand written letters from Joy "Dear" Bennett. In one of these, dated May 25, 2002, Joy expressed her amazement that so many people still remembered *Shock Theatre*, herself and Terry, but was very much concerned about correcting so much misinformation about the show and its stars circulating on the Internet.

Mostly, however, Joy was grateful for my sharing whatever memories I had about Terry with her son.

> Kerry is both touched and impressed by your interest and remembrance of his father. It has meant a lot to him. Thus, this note to mostly you!
>
> Well, you and Lyle have achieved much & now it is my turn to sit back & be impressed!! Such noteworthy accomplishments & in so many categories. How wonderful that your combined talents and unique friendship allowed those young dreams to materialize.
>
> I am sending you both a picture of Kerry, so that you can put a face [to the person] you have been communicating with. Of course, he knows none of this, but let's put it this way.... It's a mother's prerogative. Oh well, he so resembles Terry & I thought you might be interested.
>
> Take care, you two!
>
> My thoughts are with you!

And indeed, the enclosed color photo revealed Kerry's almost uncanny resemblance to his Dad.

Not long after receiving Joy's letter, on June 8, 2002, I hosted a "Memories of *Shock Theatre*" panel discussion at the "Monsters Among Us Convention" held at the Holiday Inn (now Crowne Plaza Chicago O'Hare), a hotel in the Chicago suburb of Rosemont. Lyle Conway and Rick Thomas participated on the panel, sharing information related to the show. Also on that panel, offering actual first-hand information and memories, were two surviving cast members: Bruce Newton, who played the hulking Frankenstein Monster affectionately referred to as "Shorty," and Ronny (sometimes spelled in print as Ronnie) Born, the self-proclaimed "Man of a Thousand Voices, All of Them Sounding the Same," who enacted the part of the hunchback Orville.

We invited Joy Bennett, of course, to come back to Chicago to join us on the panel. To everyone's regret, Joy, now living in Florida; was unable to attend, although in a letter she wished us all the best.

With Kerry and Joy's help, as well as assistance from Lyle, Rick, Maggie Walters and others noted in the book's acknowledgments, the present work has come together.

How fortunate I was to have met both Terry and Joy Bennett, if only briefly, on that pleasant afternoon in 1958!

I have been lucky too, in more recent years, to have befriended both Joy and Kerry through emails, letters and, once per year, Christmas cards.

I am grateful to have met and hosted that panel discussion upon which Bruce Newton and Ronny Born sat and spoke; and also to have become friends with Art

Terry Bennett's autograph, signed on the back of the official photograph (see frontispiece) sent out by WBKB-TV to fans of *Shock Theatre.*

Hern, who, as shall be shown in forthcoming pages, was a contributor in his own right to Chicago's (and *Shock Theatre*'s) history of TV horror hosts.

In the many years that have followed Chicago's *Shock Theatre*, I am fortunate to have gotten to meet — sometimes watch perform and even call friend — many folks who subsequently also played horror hosts on television and, in later years, on programs shown over the Internet, including John Zacherle (Roland and Zacherley), Fred Stuthman (Jeepers' Keeper), Lietta Harvey (Ghoulita), Jim Sullivan (Creeper), Phil Morris (Dr. Evil), Larry Vincent (Sinister Seymour), Jerry G. Bishop (Svengoolie), Rick Thomas (Lazlo, Keeper of the Dead), Ken DiGiulio (Count Midnight), Kevin Scarpino (Son of Ghoul), Maila Nurmi (Vampira), Art Hern (Drana Badour), Robert Foster (Grimsley), Jerry Moore (Karlos Borloff), Al Lewis (Grandpa), Danielle Gelehrter (Penny Dreadful), Robert Miles (Count Smokula), and last, but certainly not least, Dick Dyszel (Count Gore De Vol).

For the author this project has truly been the proverbial "trip down Memory Lane," albeit a lane populated by bloodthirsty vampires, howling werewolves, shambling mummies and a bug-eyed madman who, on live camera and with near-innocent delight, murdered or tormented his beautiful but "faceless" cohort for close to two very successful years.

The forthcoming text is based upon whatever published material I could gather as reference, much of it furnished by Kerry and Joy Bennett, Terry Tiz and Lyle Conway; and upon the first-hand memories, not always but generally accurate, of people who worked on the show.

The text is also based upon my own personal (and subjective) memories of *Shock Theatre*, some of which, having settled in my mind for over more than a half century, may have inaccuracies of their own, or may have merged with other recollections. Nonetheless, I have made every attempt to insure that what you are about to read is a more or less (the former, I hope) true account of the show and the people who worked on it, in front of the cameras, behind them or, especially in the case of Terry Bennett, both.

The journey I propose to take you on will include recalling the circumstances that led to the realization of the Windy City's answer to the nationwide "*Shock Theatre* phenomenon" and offering information on the lives and careers of the people who made Chicago's *Shock Theatre* possible (primarily Terry and Joy Bennett), and also give some sense of what it was like to watch the program and of the impact it had on so many Midwestern TV viewers.

If you watched the show and your memories of it are as strong, nostalgic and loving as my own (in other words, if you're a true "Shock Absorber," as Marvin called the show's fans), I trust the text and pictures that are to follow will, like Marvin and Dear, put at least a gruesome grin on your face. But I suspect readers of this book who actually watched *Shock Theatre* will be in the minority.

Most readers probably never saw the program, or if they did might not remember much of it, or perhaps never even heard of *Shock Theatre* at all. For you, then, this book is something more in the line of an historical document — the history of a show that for two years was an important component of Chicago television, and for a while was the top-rated local program in that city. For you, probably the majority of the readers of this book, I trust that it conveys at least some idea of what ghoulish delights so many of us enjoyed on those long-lost Saturday nights with the TV channel selector switched to seven.

Get ready and grounded — the *Shock*s are coming!

1

Off to a Shocking Start

Lightning rips across the cloudy night sky.

Ominous music plays, at first loud, fast and startling, then slow and mysterious.

Old, weathered tombstones appear; looming behind them is a once-stately, possibly haunted old mansion that reeks of evil and unseen "things."

Over the black-and-white scene come sounds of rattling chains. A skeleton (or is that a woman?) screams in terror ... screams again and again. The house is dark until light finally shows from a basement window.

Words in stark white suddenly appear over this grim tableau: SHOCK THEATRE.

The screams, still accompanied by music, continue. Then the letters shatter like glass and fall away.

Inside the house, moving away from that single lighted window, we see what appears to be a combination dungeon and mad scientist's laboratory, a place spartanly decorated with spider webs, hanging chains and an empty table.

Someone or some*thing* is slowly descending a flight of stairs. At first seen only in shadow, the figure reaches the bottom step, and then walks toward us — a young and handsome dark-haired man of modest stature, dressed entirely in black. The dark turtleneck sweater and sport jacket suggest a denizen of some darker beatnik coffee house; but the glasses — horn-rimmed with magnifying lenses — and the madly glaring eyes behind them suggest that this character may also be something else, something sinister, even fiendish.

His smile is subtle, sinister. Finally he speaks, his voice mellow yet sepulchral.

"Good evening, fiends ... er, friends," he says. "I'm Marvin. Welcome to our period of fun and relaxation, on our fun festival."

Marvin reacts to the woman's screams.

"Oh! I must apologize for the young lady's exuberance. It takes her a while to get used to me. I sort of creep up on people. Anyway, tonight we have the tender, romantic story of a boy and his love for life. Your life, my life, *anyone's life*! *Frankenstein*! The story that asks the question, 'Can a man over 35 find happiness with a playmate?' Taken from the book *How to Create Monsters for Fun and Profit*."

From some unseen part of the room, the woman moans. Turning, the man

13

Terry Bennett as Mad Marvin, the nearsighted beatnik host of *Shock Theatre*, on WBKB-TV, Channel 7, Chicago (courtesy Kerry Bennett). The Windy City saw him for the first time at 10:00 P.M. on Saturday, December 7, 1957.

who calls himself Marvin replies, "All right, Dear, I'll be with you in just a moment." Then, returning his attention to the audience, he goes on, "She's singing our song. Before we begin our heart-warming tender tale, let's have a word from the people who make me possible."

Following a commercial from a local sponsor, Marvin returns, but now he is not alone. Seated in a chair and seen only from behind is a shapely, seemingly attractive (we can't be certain, because we cannot see her face) young woman. Marvin is holding her hand.

"I'm glad you're feeling better, my Dear. You see it only hurts for a little while. And now, for *Frankenstein*, the story of what a boy can do with perseverance, ability and a king-size Erector set."

Releasing the woman's hand, he says, "Our story begins with a rope, and as any hangman will tell you, anything that has a rope in it is wonderful. This, then, is the story...."

—✠—

With those softly spoken words, uttered by a gnomish and bespectacled man in black, the original *Frankenstein*, made 26 years before by Universal Pictures but this night having its Chicago television debut, began. No opening credits were shown, as would be the norm for movies yet to come. The scene went directly from Marvin to the opening scene of the movie.

The movie, *Frankenstein*, was a *bona fide* classic of the genre, a kind of prototype movie that, following *Dracula* made earlier the same year (1931), would launch the first great wave of sound-era horror movies. The motion picture's story was a familiar one. Based loosely on the novel by Mary Wollstonecraft Shelley, first published in 1818, the movie told the tale of Henry Frankenstein (played by Colin Clive), an overly ambitious scientist who creates a Monster (Boris Karloff) from parts of different corpses and then brings it to life via electricity. The Monster, possessing a criminal's brain, proceeds to cause havoc until eventually turning on his creator.

Many Chicagoans watching Channel 7 that night were seeing *Frankenstein* for the first time; also, starting at 10:00 P.M. that cool night of December 7, 1957, they were being fed their first taste of a new Saturday night series of old horror movies. The show was called *Shock Theatre and* Marvin was the "horror host" who introduced those movies.

Getting to Know Marvin

Chicago's *Shock Theatre* was not the first program in the United States to call itself by that name. But, like most others, it was a 90-minute show, the perfect length to accommodate *Frankenstein* as well as subsequent movies, most of which had running times of approximately 70 minutes. Thus, a 90-minute timeslot could include the movie, plus various commercials and also a series of skits featuring Marvin and, more often than not, his sexy foil.

On this debut night, the first commercial break occurred during the famous laboratory scene wherein Henry Frankenstein and his hunchbacked assistant Fritz (played by Dwight Frye) bring the Monster to life:

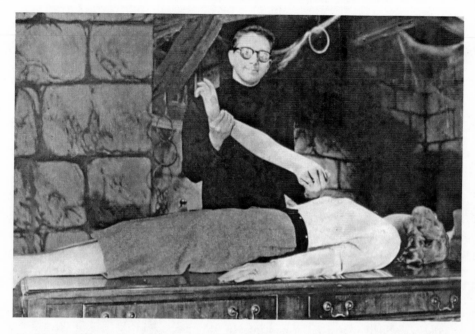

Marvin (Terry Bennett) demonstrates that he is in favor of disarmament on December 7, 1957, the first night that *Shock Theatre* aired. "Dear," whose face was never shown on the program, is here played by model Dorothy Johnson.

Dear (AKA "Her"), the young woman whose face is never seen, is lying on her back on the table, her head turned away from camera. Marvin, standing beside the table, removes one of her arms (a prop, naturally).

"Someone threw the wrong switch," Marvin quips, raising high the dismembered limb. "I'm back again. I should mention that Dr. Frankenstein was banned by the American Medical Society. They thought he shouldn't be wasting time creating monsters when he should be out testing cigarettes. But now, someone in the laboratory has a word for you. Let's give him a big hand."

Dear moans, obviously not pleased with losing an arm.

Marvin admonishes her. "Pull yourself together."

Frankenstein had several additional breaks, each time with. Marvin returning to put Dear through some new torment.

"Isn't that story wonderful? You know it was filmed with such realism that the director killed himself. It adds something. Let's pause now ... for a breather."

To some viewers lacking a macabre sense of humor, it must have seemed blasphemous interrupting a classic motion picture like *Frankenstein* with such lowbrow comedy bits. Probably the intent of most people who had decided to tune in *Shock Theatre* on that opening night was simply to watch the movie.

But many viewers found Marvin's antics as entertaining — perhaps even more so — than the film itself. Certainly *Frankenstein* was a critically acclaimed masterpiece of its type; but it was, after all, an old movie, rather creaky in some scenes, and lacking a music score, and may have seemed to some viewers accustomed to more rapidly paced fare even somewhat boring. Indeed, as *Frankenstein* progressed toward its climax, some viewers mostly likely anticipated and welcomed Marvin's interruptions. When *Frankenstein* ended, with the Monster meeting his demise in a burning windmill, Marvin returned pulling a heavy locked trunk across the cellar floor.

> "Oh, he was such a nice boy, too," says Marvin of the ill-fated Monster. "He had a wonderful future in front of him. See what happens when you play with matches? But next week, we've got a beautiful comedy to look forward to. Let's take a look at it...."
>
> The scene switches to a coming attractions trailer for from next week's movie, another Universal Pictures horror classic: *The Wolf Man*, starring Lon Chaney, Jr. and Bela Lugosi. The preview over, Marvin directs his attention again to the trunk.
>
> "The young lady is taking a trip and I helped her pack her *Wolf Man* ... direct from the Lincoln Park Zoo. And now I've got to go. I've been invited to a shocktail party. And, oh yes, when you have your shocktail party, be sure to serve Bloody Marys."
>
> Then, to the trunk, he says, "Say good night to the people."

Chicago TV viewers had met Marvin (sometimes referred to as Mad Marvin). To most viewers who tuned in that night, he was a pleasant surprise. Many of them would come back the following week, looking forward to a second dose of his unique blend of horror and humor as much as they anticipated seeing *The Wolf Man*.

Three Stations Named WBKB

Locally produced television programs were an important part of TV history — unlike the situation today, where most local programming is devoted to news shows and sporting events. During the late 1950s every major city had its own local stations, each with its individual line-up of original shows. Chicago's *Shock Theatre* was such a program.

Yet Chicago's *Shock Theatre* was not the first local television program going by that name and running old horror movies like *Frankenstein* and *The Wolf Man*; nor was Marvin the first of the breed who would come to be known as TV "horror hosts." Taken together, they were, in fact, responses of local television station WBKB-TV (Channel 7), the city's affiliate of the ABC-TV network, to several nationwide phenomena that had been occurring during the mid–50s.

Actually, there have been three local television stations that went by the call letters of WBKB, one of them a CBS affiliate currently operating out of Alpena, Michigan. The first WBKB was a pioneering local station that first aired, over Channel 4, in 1940. Distinguished as Chicago's first commercial television station, this original WBKB was developed and nurtured by an ex-submarine skipper named Captain William Crawford "Bill" Eddy.

Very little programming emerged from that WBKB's studios in the station's earliest days. By the mid–40s, however, the station's empty timeslots began filling up with local personalities. Mostly thanks to Eddy's efforts, viewers of the original WBKB were soon able to watch the likes of Hugh Downs and Mike Wallace reading the news. The station also offered local boxing bouts and wrestling matches. It wasn't long before this WBKB could claim to be the first Chicago station to broadcast games starring the city's beloved baseball team, the Cubs.

Always open to ideas and interviewing new talent, WBKB provided breakthrough opportunities for talent awaiting a chance to prove themselves. Among the newcomers who would get their start at WBKB was Eddy's friend Burr Tillstrom, who in 1948 would premiere on the station his classic puppet show *Kukla, Fran and Ollie*.

In 1953, five years following Eddy's departure from the station over numerous differences of opinion, WBKB became part of a package deal in which the local station was bought by another network, CBS. Included in this transaction, moving over to CBS, was much of WBKB's talent. It wasn't long, however, before CBS would change the name of its Chicago affiliate, airing over Channel 2, to WBBM-TV.

Another local Chicago station at the time was WENR-TV. The city's ABC-TV affiliate, it could be seen on Channel 7. With the original WBKB at CBS and renamed WBBM, the former call letters were free to be used. Thus, WENR-TV changed its name to WBKB, one that was already familiar to Chicagoans owning television sets. The Channel 7 station retained those call letters until 1968 when the station was once more renamed, his time WLS-TV.

Back in the Fifties...

Shock Theatre's Windy City premiere was heralded in the local edition of *TV Guide* magazine, which hit the newsstands on the morning of Monday,

December 2. The issue included a nice full-page advertisement announcing the program's name and the movie to be shown that night. The ad featured a full-face front view of the Frankenstein Monster.

That same *TV Guide* advertisement, or slight variants of it, would also appear on Saturday, the day *Frankenstein* would debut on TV, in other local publications including the city's three main largest newspapers, the *Chicago Sun-Times,* the *Chicago Daily News* and the *Chicago American.*

The description of *Frankenstein* in that *TV Guide* issue gave a few more plot details (although the release date given was also off by one year) than did the one in the *Sun-Times* guidebook:

"Frankenstein."
(1932) Chgo. TV Debut. A young scientist has fashioned a human body and is conducting experiments to see if he can make it come to life. His fiancée and his friends try to stop him, but to no avail. From the novel by Mary Shelley.

As if afraid to use the term "horror," *TV Guide* labeled *Frankenstein,* and all the movies subsequently shown on *Shock Theatre,* a melodrama.

It's doubtful that many Chicagoans who saw those ads realized

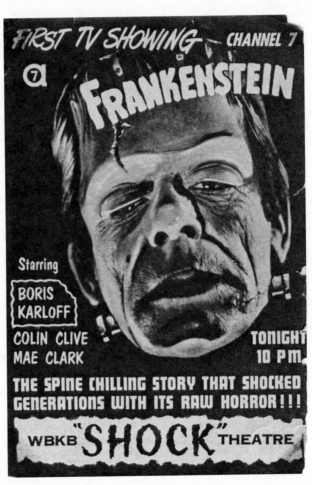

Full-page advertisement for the premiere of Chicago's *Shock Theatre,* published in *TV Guide* magazine. The movie that night was the 1931 *Frankenstein* but the ad features a picture of Glenn Strange rather than *Frankenstein* star Boris Karloff as the Monster. Variations of this ad also appeared in the local newspapers.

that the Monster's face depicted was not that of Boris Karloff, but was instead that of one of the actor's successors, Glenn Strange, from the 1948 comedy-horror film *Abbott and Costello Meet Frankenstein*, which would *not* be ever shown on the series.

Shock Theatre was a product of the 1950s, and the year 1957 was an ideal one to debut the program. The Fifties constituted a period of change in the United States and much of the changes the country was experiencing by the middle of that decade concerned young people and their attitudes toward adults and symbols of adult authority.

Rock 'n' roll music was still raw and in its infancy, something to accept or reject. For some teenagers, the appeal of the music was in the fact that most parents hated it (unlike today, when, after more than a half century, the genre has become mainstream and the music of parents and grandparents). Performers like Elvis "The Pelvis" Presley, Little Richard and Jerry Lee Lewis were raising both the eyebrows and ire of religious and censorship groups and were even considered, by some adults, dangerous.

Mad magazine, then publishing what today might be called "cutting edge" humor, was for many teenagers and young adults their new popular culture bible. The satire magazine, to be much imitated at the time by a flood of mostly inferior competitors, attacked current taboos and exposed hypocrisies. And its dimwitted mascot Alfred E, Newman became a much beloved anti-establishment symbol and antihero for young American readers.

There were countless horror comic books, with titles like *The Vault of Horror, Chamber of Chills* and even *Frankenstein*. Many of their stories featured such traditional horror figures as vampires, zombies, werewolves and ghouls, some of them depicting in four colors the most gruesome imagery conceivable and all of them selling for a dime. They were the most popular periodicals on newsstands among children and teens until pressure groups, spearheaded by psychiatrist Dr. Frederick Wertham mostly via his 1954 best-selling book *Seduction of the Innocent,* put them out of business by the end of that same year. According to Dr. Wertham's sensationalize treatise, young people who read such "trash" became juvenile delinquents.

Juvenile delinquency, which had increased on the country's streets dramatically following the end of World War II, was making newspaper headlines and was a frequent topic discussed on radio and television and in books and magazine articles. The "JD" image was a popular one, attractive to myriad teenagers. Many teenage boys, even though not themselves delinquents, followed the motion picture images of Marlon Brando, James Dean and Elvis, greasing up and slicking back their hair while clad in jeans and black leather jackets.

In the past, werewolves, Frankenstein creatures and vampires, as portrayed in movies, had been depicted strictly as adult characters. By the time 1957 came around, however, adolescent versions of such classic horrors were appearing on motion picture screens. Movies with titles like *I Was a Teenage Werewolf*, *I Was a Teenage Frankenstein* and *Blood of Dracula* were immediate hits. For once teenagers could relate to — even empathize with — monsters their own age.

People lived in fear during the 1950s, not of Teenage Werewolves and Teenage Frankensteins, but of their own annihilation. The Cold War was being waged at full force, with both sides — us and "them" — in constant dread of the other being first to drop that latest-model atomic bomb. Paranoia was rampant, with Communists presumably lurking under beds. The world seemed utterly bleak to many a young person of the '50s. Some of them, seeing only futility in their lives and nothing in their future, removed themselves from general society, taking refuge with the growing Beat Generation.

Compensating for some of this paranoia, so-called "sick" comedians, like Mort Sahl and Dick Gregory, mixing political commentary with their humor, became the rage in nightclubs; and what were known as "sick jokes" and "shut-up" jokes (and sometimes marriages of the two) spread through every schoolyard:

"But Mommy, I hate my sister's guts."
"Shut up, kid, and eat what I give you!"

The so-called "beatnik movement" in the '50s constituted the prevailing venue for counter-culture self-expression and rebellion. In coffee houses, "beat" poets, artists, musicians and other creative types gathered and shared their work and their often radical ideas. Beatniks rebelled against "The Establishment," sometimes through their creative works, and purported to be nonconformists, although many of them, wearing beards and clad in black, were, at least visually, difficult to tell apart.

It became fashionable for young people, whether or not they were actual "beats," to adopt the garb and jargon of the "hip" denizens of such haunts, with basic black being the color of choice.

Young people were gravitating towards the changes occurring around them and rebelling against the status quo, much to the chagrin of their parents and other people of authority. The atmosphere — darker, even more sinister than before — was just right for receiving a new show like *Shock Theatre*. It was in just such an atmosphere that the character of the ebony-clad Marvin — Chicago's hippest and darkest beatnik — was born.

Marvin was, in fact, the apex in nonconformity and rebellion; indeed, he was Chicago's *ultimate* beatnik antihero.

"Gothic" Horrors Return — Sort Of

UFO sightings were commonly reported in the 1950s and the dread of nuclear war had become the era's Sword of Damocles. Thus, capitalizing on the public's contemporary concerns, movies made about monsters during the '50s were mostly of the science fiction genre, with such creatures as giant bugs, rampaging dinosaurs and mutated humans usually having extraterrestrial- or atom-based origins.

Yet other changes were occurring in the '50s, at least in regards to Hollywood movies — a growing resurgence of interest in horror movies of the "old school." Following about a half decade of motion pictures about creatures from outer space or spawned in atomic tests, the motion picture industry began — for whatever reason — to rediscover monsters whose origins were rooted more in legends, curses and Gothic castles than on other planets or the splitting of an atom. Indeed, some of the movies that would emerge from Hollywood during the mid–50s seemed to be throwbacks to what the studios had been making decades earlier.

The first of this new wave of "old style" monster movies was *Bride of the Monster*, produced, written and directed by Edward D. Wood, Jr. (of *Plan 9 from Outer Space* infamy). Released in May 1955, this cheaply made independent film starred Bela Lugosi, whose name would appear in the credits of numerous movies shown later on *Shock Theatre*. The movie harkened back to the mad scientist movies made by Poverty Row companies like Monogram and PRC during the 1940s, some of them also with Lugosi.

In *Bride of the Monster*, Lugosi portrayed a mad scientist who, aided by a hulking and lumbering servant (played by Tor Johnson), tries to create a "race of atomic supermen," but succeeds only in killing his human guinea pigs. As in so many films of past decades, Lugosi's character fell victim to his own weird experiments, becoming the very "superman" — but also a monster — he'd for so long tried to create. Although the movie had an atomic power–based origin and climaxed with a stock shot of an exploding A-bomb, its old dark house setting and mad doctor's laboratory suggested a kind of movie that hadn't been made in years.

Bride of the Monster—like some of the better horror films in which Bela Lugosi appeared — would later be shown on Chicago's version of *Shock Theatre*. Certainly not to suggest that *Bride of the Monster* was any kind of inspiration, but more "old-fashioned" horror outings were released the following year. These included *Indestructible Man* (March, 1956), starring Lon Chaney, Jr. as an executed killer revived from the dead, who then avenges himself on his former enemies (a movie similar to *Man Made Monster*, an older Chaney movie that would play on *Shock Theatre*); *The Black Sleep* (June, 1956), featuring horror veterans Basil Rathbone, Chaney, Lugosi, John Carradine and newcomer Tor Johnson, about an obsessed scientist trying to cure his wife via brain-surgery experiments, producing instead (not surprisingly) a horde of mad or hideous creatures; and *The Werewolf* (July 1956), a Columbia Pictures film that, as discussed in the forthcoming section, may have played a role in the steps leading up to *Shock Theatre*.

More significant, however, at least in terms of sheer numbers, were some of the next year's horror offerings, including *The Curse of Frankenstein* (June, 1957), a retelling of the famous Mary Shelley theme, this time in full and graphic color, and introducing two new horror stars to the genre, Peter Cushing as Baron Frankenstein and Christopher Lee as the Creature; *I Was a Teenage Werewolf* (June, 1957), in which a mad doctor uses a combination of drugs and hypnosis to revert a troubled high school student to a primitive lupine state; *The Vampire* (July, 1957), wherein another doctor accidentally takes pills that regress him into a vampire-like creature needing human blood to survive; and, released on November 23 (coincidentally Boris Karloff's birthday), just one month before *Shock Theatre* debuted, the double-bill of *I Was a Teenage Frankenstein*, in which a descendant of the original monster-making scientist creates a new monster from parts of dead teenagers, and *Blood of Dracula*, wherein a student at an all-girls school is transformed by a teacher, using an ancient medallion and hypnosis, into a human vampire.

Apparently the companies that released these films were still not entirely confident that the "old school" monsters could succeed in the modern world based solely on their own merits. Indeed, most of these features went to theatres co-billed with standard-issue science-fiction fare: *The Werewolf*, for example, went out on a double-bill with *Earth vs. the Flying Saucers*, in which Washington, D.C. is attacked by invaders from outer space; *The Vampire* was co-featured with *The Monster That Challenged the World*, about giant prehistoric snails; and *I Was a Teenage Werewolf* was coupled with the SF comedy *Invasion of the Saucer Men*.

More notably, the majority of these movies, when featuring a creature traditionally associated with mythology or the supernatural (*e.g.*, *The Vampire*, *I Was a Teenage Werewolf*), now had science to explain their origins.

Realart *and* The Werewolf

The *authentic* old-fashioned horror motion pictures — the ones made by Universal Pictures in the 1930s and 1940s featuring the original Frankenstein Monster, Count Dracula, Wolf Man, Mummy and other iconic horrors —

were far from missing in action in the public's consciousness during the 1950s. Those movies would continue to play in Chicago neighborhood theatres like the Alex, the Modé and the Biograph (wheré Public Enemy No. 1 John Dillinger was shot to death on July 22, 1934, by FBI agents), often on double or even triple bills, through the early months of the year of *Shock Theatre*'s premiere.

After 1946, the year that Universal Pictures morphed into the more prestigious Universal-International, the studio made available for reissue distribution its old movies. Realart Pictures, Inc., a company founded in 1948 by Jack Broder and Joe Harris, leased many of the movies in Universal's library, including the horror titles, on a ten-year basis. Realart then made the pictures available to neighborhood theatres, with a habit of removing Universal's opening label and splicing on their own (two reels, with film spooling from one to the other) and leaving some people, not familiar with the history of these old movies, with the impression that Realart had actually made them.

While Realart was handling the old Universal movies, it was no surprise for a reader to open the morning newspaper, page through to the entertainment section, then find a double bill of *The Ghost of Frankenstein* and *Dead Man's Eyes* playing at some out-of-the way drive-in theatre, or a triple horror show combining *House of Frankenstein, House of Dracula* and *The Mummy* playing over a weekend at some rundown neighborhood movie house.

Following their lengthy association with Realart, Universal-International noted the value in their old monsters. In 1957, United World Films, a subsidiary of Universal-International, made a number of them available for home rental in the 16mm format. These included all the Frankenstein, Dracula, Wolf Man, Mummy and Invisible Man series, along with the later comedy-horror entries including Bud Abbott and Lou Costello produced under the Universal-International banner. To promote rentals of the old movies, United World produced a nice brochure, complete with photos of some of their famed monsters.

As already noted, Columbia Pictures released a movie in the mid–50s titled simply *The Werewolf.* The movie was released in July 1956, a time when Realart's reissues, including films featuring Lon Chaney, Jr. as the original Wolf Man character, were still getting theatrical circulation. *The Werewolf* followed the basic theme of Universal's Wolf Man movies, *i.e.,* a man, through circumstances beyond his control, is transformed into a human beast, a hybrid of man and wolf. Depressed, hating what Fate has dealt him, he seeks either a cure or death — anything that might suppress or end his desire to kill. (Lawrence Talbot, the doomed character played by Chaney, becomes a werewolf because of a Gypsy curse, assumed when he survives a bite of another werewolf [played in the original *Wolf Man* by Bela Lugosi].)

Duncan Marsh (Steven Ritch), the title character of *The Werewolf*, has a different kind of origin — one based, in keeping with the sensibilities of the 1950s, i.e., in science rather than the supernatural. Marsh's condition is the result of two misguided scientists injecting him with a serum derived from wolf's blood. The scientists' reason for doing this is a simple (and maybe plausible) one, given when the movie was made: They believed that through their experimentation, mankind might be able to survive the resulting radiation of a nuclear attack.

Taking into account the other kinds of monster movies being made in 1956, *The Werewolf* was an odd title to turn up in advertisements. This was, after all, a werewolf movie. And a *new* werewolf motion picture had not been released in the United States since 1948; and that movie was a comedy, *Abbott and Costello Meet Frankenstein.* Might the Columbia organization been more or less "testing the waters," experimenting to determine how a 1940s–type horror character, albeit with its updated science-founded origin, would play with a modern audience?

Steven Ritch in *The Werewolf*, a 1956 horror movie from Columbia Pictures, gave a science fiction spin to a more or less traditional horror theme. Possibly the success of this movie, with its iconic monster figure, played a role in Columbia's subdivision Screen Gems' decision to release some of Universal Pictures old horror movies, some of them about werewolves, to television the following year.

Indeed, was *The Werewolf* a kind of "trial run" on Columbia's part; and were company executives pondering that if a movie about a man transforming into a "wolf man," like Lon Chaney did back in the 1940s, did well on large theatre screens, maybe the same kind of movie — indeed, a series of them, already made and ready to show — could attract even a possibly larger audience on the small home screen?.

One can only speculate if there were any cause and effect connection between the box office receipts for Columbia's *Werewolf* and what would soon follow.

Screen Gems' Shock! *Package*

Screen Gems was a subsidiary branch of Columbia Pictures that packaged and released older movies to television.

The same year that Columbia Pictures released *The Werewolf,* Screen Gems secured the television rights to 600 old (pre–1948) movies made by Universal Pictures, and Universal-International, including those featuring Chaney's Wolf Man. With Screen Gems' new deal and Realart's lease with Universal-International now terminated, the old movies featuring Frankenstein's Monster, Dracula and other horror characters were no longer being shown theatrically.

The following year, possibly because of the current successes of the new but old-style horror films being turned out by Hollywood production companies, and also the recent track records of Realart's reissues of the original Universal product, Screen Gems put together a package of 52 movies (one for each week) under the umbrella title of *Shock!*

To promote the availability of these films for TV broadcast, Screen Gems produced a large, horizontally oriented book with the same name as the film package. The *Shock!* book listed each of the 52 moves, along with a photo from the film, its basic credits and a plot synopsis. Screen Gems sent copies of the book to local stations to create interest in purchasing the film package. Additionally, Screen Gems provided, both to potential buyers and also to magazines that might publicize the package, sets of 8x10 still photographs, one per movie title.

Most but not all of the *Shock!* package titles (listed below in alphabetical order) were horror films:

The Black Cat (1934)	*Dead Man's Eyes* (1945)
Calling Dr. Death (1943)	*Destination Unknown* (1942)
The Cat Creeps (1946)	*Dracula* (1931)
Chinatown Squad (1935)	*Dracula's Daughter* (1936)
Danger Woman (1946)	*Enemy Agent* (1940)
A Dangerous Game (1941)	*Frankenstein* (1931)

Frankenstein Meets the Wolf Man (1943)
The Frozen Ghost (1945)
The Great Impersonation (1935)
Horror Island (1941)
House of Horrors (1946)
The Invisible Man (1933)
The Invisible Man Returns (1940)
The Invisible Ray (1936)
The Last Warning (1938)
The Mad Doctor of Market Street (1942)
The Mad Ghoul (1943)
Man Made Monster (1941)
The Man Who Cried Wolf (1937)
The Mummy (1933)
The Mummy's Ghost (1944)
The Mummy's Hand (1940)
The Mummy's Tomb (1942)
Murders in the Rue Morgue (1932)
Mystery of Edwin Drood (1935)

Mystery of Marie Roget (1942)
Mystery of the White Room (1939)
Night Key (1937)
Night Monster (1942)
Nightmare (1942)
Pillow of Death (1945)
The Raven (1935)
Reported Missing (1937)
Sealed Lips (1941)
Secret of the Blue Room (1933)
Secret of the Chateau (1934)
She-Wolf of London (1946)
Son of Dracula (1943)
Son of Frankenstein (1939)
The Spider Woman Strikes Back (1946)
The Spy Ring (1938)
The Strange Case of Doctor Rx (1942)
Weird Woman (1944)
WereWolf of London (1935)
The Witness Vanishes (1939)
The Wolf Man (1941)

The reason why such bona fide horror movies as *The Ghost of Frankenstein*, *House of Dracula* and *The Mummy's Curse* were *not* included in the package, while such mundane titles as *Danger Woman*, *Chinatown Squad* and *The Witness Vanishes* were, remains unclear. Perhaps one or both companies were reserving them with an eye towards the future?

High-Voltage Shocks = High Ratings

Screen Gems' *Shock!* package proved to be immediately — and immensely — a hit.

According to Ted Okuda and Mark Yurkiw, in their 2007 book *Chicago TV Horror Movie Show: From Shock Theatre to Svengoolie* (essential reading for people interested in Chicago's long history of TV horror hosts), the package was sold in 142 local television stations across the country for late-night showings. Most but not all stations that bought the Screen Gems bundle tended to name their local shows after the package itself, with myriad programs titled *Shock Theatre* springing up, each with its own unique horror host character.

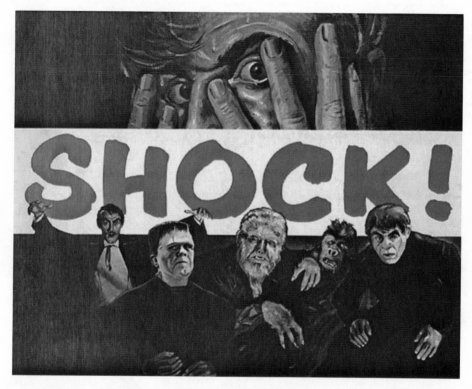

Screen Gems sent this promotional booklet to local television stations across America in hopes of selling them its package of 52 *Shock!* movies. Today this publication is a highly sought after (and expensive) item among collectors of horror movie and TV memorabilia.

"At first, the films were broadcast by themselves," wrote Okuda and Yurkiw, "until stations decided to feature live hosts to introduce the movies and perform skits between commercial breaks."

Horror hosts began cropping up in one American city after another. Often these characters appeared courtesy of some already employed studio staff member of modest or even questionable talent, perhaps a floor manager or TV weatherman, coaxed, bribed or threatened into donning some weird disguise, often wearing heavy fright makeup. Sometimes a virtually shanghaied non-performer was required to write his or her own material and apply his or her own makeup, the results for either not always being professional.

Among the first, most popular and best of these pioneering *Shock Theatre* hosts was John Zacherle, who debuted at 11:15 P.M. on Monday, October 7, on Philadelphia local station WCAU-TV. Zacherle appeared that night as the sinister yet amusing Roland, described as the "Cool Ghoul." Roland sported the nineteenth-century outfit Zacherle had worn when playing a nutty undertaker on an earlier local Western show called *Action in the After-noon.*

As would other horror hosts, Roland introduced the old horror movies, interrupting them at various times to do horror-themed skits, sometimes even inserting himself into the films to converse with the characters or participate in the action. At the end of his shows, Roland would cheerfully give viewers his trademark farewell: "Good night ... *whatever* you are!"

Zacherle would move soon his show to New York, where he called himself the newly spelled Zacherley. He soon spread his talents over to recordings (his double-sided "Dinner with Drac" 45 RPM record would hit the popular-music charts), both "singles" and albums, and radio, television and live personal appearances.

John Zacherle was one of the first "horror hosts" to show the *Shock!* films, predating the Chicago show by two months. Although his character is best known as simply Zacherle, he began as Roland, the Cool Ghoul, on local Philadelphia station WCAU-TV (courtesy John Zacherle).

Wherever the *Shock!* movies played on television, ratings for those stations soared overnight. New York's WABC-TV, never in its history number one in its Thursday 11:15 P.M. time spot, jumped to that position that night with its premiere of the original *Dracula* starring Bela Lugosi. Ratings for the station increased from a lowly 1.6 and a 9.5 percent share to a spectacular 8.8 rating and a 41.7 percent share. Similar ratings hikes occurred in Philadelphia for Zacherle's show, also for Los Angeles' KTLA-TV, premiering October 1 at 9:30, San Francisco's KRON-TV, premiering October 3 at 10:30, and

San Antonio's KENS-TV, premiering October 4 at 10:00, all starting off with *Frankenstein*.

By the time the *Shock Theatre* format arrived in Chicago TV there were shows with that name playing in at least a half dozen other major U.S. cities.

Like Frankenstein's Monster in his first broadcast movie, *Shock Theatre* roared to electronical life in Chicago that seventh night of December 1957. But like other aspects of the Windy City, including the Cubs baseball team, deep-dish pizza and local machine-run politics, Chicago's *Shock Theatre* would have a style all its own.

And for a while, at least, that show — and its host, the maniacal Marvin — were there to stay.

2

Initial Shocks

Dear falls into a slump. Is she dead?

"She takes the strangest times to take a nap," says Marvin, standing in his dungeon domain near a glass marked "Embalming Fluid," looking towards the woman. He tsk- tsks; then, reacting with a start to his audience, he goes on, "Oh, hello! I'm Marvin, your ghost ... er, host! You can call me Marv, for short. You may not be around for long."

The young woman moans. Marvin shakes his head.

"There she goes, talking in her sleep again! Anyway, tonight we have another comedy for you. Our story is called *The Wolf Man*. And this is the original *Wolf Man*, not the cheap imitations like the ones you meet at Christmas parties. Which reminds me of the last monster party I went to. Everyone was there and we had a wonderful time. We sat around and cut our wrists. Oh, that reminds me. I would like to thank [mentions a viewer's name] for the sample of what he served at his last shocktail party. I already sipped a little of it ... and it's really a stiff drink."

He sips from the glass. "Here's blood in your eye!"

Again the woman groans.

"Nag, nag, nag," Marvin goes on, "that's all she does! Little people in the laboratory are working, so let's take a look at their creations, shall we."

Following the first commercial, Marvin is back, caught in the act of using pliers to yank off Dear's fingernails.

"There, that wasn't so bad, was it?" he assures her. "You did ask for a manicure, didn't you? Oh, well, just be patient. And now for *The Wolf Man* ... the story of a man who looked sharp, felt sharp and was sharp ... but still wasn't fixed for blades. Perhaps we'd better explain how a man can turn into a wolf. For this we'll consult the encyclopedia and, by a strange coincidence, this leads us to our story..."

The image on the television screen changed to the opening shot in *The Wolf Man*, showing someone else's hand removing a large book from its shelf. Thus, on December 14, began the second telecast of *Shock Theatre*.

TV Guide advertisement for the second movie shown on *Shock Theatre.*

—ᗰ—

Around the time *The Wolf Man* showed on *Shock Theatre*, the black-clad man behind the thick glasses explained his *modus operandi* to an uncredited *Chicago Sun-Times* reporter. "I'm supposed to do for this show what Charles Addams does in the *New Yorker*," Terry Bennett said, "satirize death, even make you laugh at it. I have to provide a natural segue from live TV into the film shock. How? By doing maniacal things, but looking like I think it's all perfectly sensible."

To many viewers of Chicago's *Shock Theatre*, the madman named Marvin was the only horror host around.

But Marvin certainly wasn't the first of his breed. John Zacherle and other TV horror hosts, both male and female, were already introducing the *Shock!* movies and performing skits by the time Bennett first strode down the stairs of his dungeon set. There were characters with names like Gorgon (Bill Camfield, a ghoulish-looking guy on a show named *Nightmare*, operating out of KFJZ in Dallas–Fort Worth, Texas) and Tarantula Ghoul (Suzanne Waldron as a sexy *femme fatale* on *House of Horror*, KPTV, Portland, Oregon).

The horror host concept had, in fact, already enjoyed a lengthy tradition in media outside of television decades before anyone at Screen Gems ever thought of compiling that original *Shock!* package. The basic idea behind horror host–type characters seems rooted in live theatre followed by early motion pictures, wherein scenes of comedy relief were routinely interjected into a mystery (as horror plays and films were once labeled), to ease for audience members the tension caused by a suspenseful story. *Dracula*, for example, in both its Broadway play and subsequent Universal movie versions, included such comedic scenes for the purposes of counterbalancing the more intense and frightening scenes in its story of a human vampire.

Competition from MGM?

Shock Theatre was an instant hit.

Naturally, however, the show had its competition. And until the debut of *Shock Theatre*, there really was no competition for Chicago's 10:00 P.M. Saturday TV timeslot.

Shock Theatre had been scheduled directly opposite WBBM Channel 2's top-rated *The Best of MGM*, which ran on a weekly basis motion pictures of a decidedly higher caliber than most if not all of what Marvin would be screening. Interestingly, just weeks before *Shock Theatre* debuted with *Frankenstein*, the Channel 2 series had shown for the first time on Chicago television a classic horror movie in its own library, MGM's 1941 glossy version of *Dr. Jekyll and Mr. Hyde* starring Spencer Tracy.

The top brass at WBBM quickly took note of *Shock Theatre*'s high ratings. Viewers who had been regularly turning their channel selectors each Saturday night at 10 o'clock to watch some high-budget movie starring Tracy, Clark Gable or Myrna Loy were now switching over to Channel 7 to see the latest offering featuring Boris Karloff, Bela Lugosi or Lon Chaney, Jr. Something needed to be done to bring back those former MGM movie viewers.

What was attracting viewers to *Shock Theatre*? Surely it couldn't be the motion pictures themselves, many of them just "B" movies or "programmers"! Noting that the Channel 7 show had a comedic host, the WBBM powers-that-be decided to follow the example of its new and still young competition. Yes, the Channel 2 top brass must have thought, Marvin was the reason that they were losing much of their audience.

In retaliation, WBBM hired, at least as an experiment, well-known radio and motion picture comedian Jerry Colonna to host the MGM movies. The plan at Channel 2 was that the popular Colonna had the star (and comedic) power to lure away some of Terry Bennett's viewers.

In his first appearance on the WBBM show, Colonna sat in a director's chair, mimicking the role of a Hollywood film producer-director. As described in a *Chicago Sun-Times* article, "Chi Stages Late Night Film War," appearing during the week following *Shock Theatre*'s premiere:

> As a typical gimmick, on his opening night, [Colonna's] picked up talking about Hollywood really being a very normal place, then stands up revealing an outlandish costume. From a desk drawer, he removes a can of film, blows the dust off and throws the reel out a window with a trademark cue. "Roll it, Dudley." Then the film goes on. Colonna also serves as an entertaining bridge into the commercials, designed to discourage viewers from running out to the kitchen.

Whether or not Colonna could have beaten Bennett in popularity and ratings (or would have been funnier) can never be known. After just that first week trying out his movie-hosting job, Colonna departed, having already committed to an overseas tour with his friend Bob Hope.

Horror Hosts Only Heard

The actual horror host phenomenon — whereby a strange or mysterious character introduced (but didn't actually participate in) a tale of suspense, mystery or outright horror, sometimes speaking lines flavored with dark humor — began on dramatic radio. Unlike the TV horror hosts yet to come, most notably those of the *Shock!* films era, these radio storytellers originated on the networks of their day rather than on local stations.

The Shadow, one of radio's most famous and popular characters, seems to have been the prototype for what would eventually evolve into the television horror host.

Two years before The Shadow began "clouding men's minds so they cannot see him" in his one-man crusade against crime on his own program, which would appropriately be titled *The Shadow*, the character (originally played by James La Curto) was only a narrator — a mysterious voice that, on the CBS series *Detective Story Hour* (1930–31), introduced mystery stories dramatized from the pages of Street and Smith Publications' *Detective Story Magazine*. The format was retained, with Frank Readick, Jr., voicing The Shadow's words, on two subsequent CBS programs, *Blue Coal Revue* (1931–32) and, oddly enough, *Love Story Drama* (1931–1932), the latter later renamed *Love Story Hour*.

This format promptly carried over to the motion picture screen when, in 1931, the same year it released *Frankenstein*, Universal Pictures introduced its "Shadow Detective Series" comprising a half dozen short films adapted from tales published in *Detective Story Magazine*. The films, like the radio shows, were introduced by The Shadow. (Later Shadow movies would feature the character as a protagonist, not just a narrator.)

The Shadow may have been an inspiration to writers for and producers of other early dramatic radio shows. Not long after his airwave debut, similar mysterious characters were introducing stories of mystery, suspense and crime, indeed even horror and science fiction.

The earliest radio series presenting all-out horror stories hosted by a weird character appears to have been *The Witch's Tale*, which began on the Mutual network in 1931. The show was originally written and directed by Alonzo Deen Cole, his scripts influenced by stories currently appearing in the cheaply produced pulp magazines, a main source of popular entertainment of the era. It was hosted by a character named Old Nancy (first voiced on the show by stage actress Adelaid Fitz-Allan).

The Hermit's Cave was a mid–1930s anthology series syndicated by station WJR in Detroit, featuring a cackling character (first played by John Kent) not unlike some of the later ghoulish TV personalities. The eerie-sounding old Hermit introduced each episode: "Ghost stories, weird stories and murder, too. The Hermit knows of them all. Turn out your lights, turn them out! Ahhhhh, have you heard the story...? Then listen, while the Hermit tells you the story."

In 1942, two CBS anthology programs, both more prestigious than *The Witch's Tale* and *The Hermit's Cave*, featured more serious-sounding host characters. The excellent *Suspense* prefaced each story with an introduction by the mostly humorless Man in Black (voiced by Joe Kearns). The titled character of *The Whistler* (originally portrayed by Bill Forman) not only introduced the show's dramatized story, but, like Marvin and so many other TV horror hosts of future years, occasionally interrupted them, oftentimes interjecting subjective comments about what was transpiring in the tale. Both *Suspense* and *The Whistler* sometimes deviated from the more mundane mystery format by delving into horror, science fiction and fantasy.

Like his predecessor The Shadow, the Whistler continued his role as mysterious narrator on the motion picture screen, appearing only as a shadow on the wall or pavement, in a series of low-budget programmers released by Columbia Pictures from 1944 to 1948. In most of these Whistler films, actor Richard Dix starred as the protagonist. Both *Suspense* and *The Whistler* would eventually also move to television.

The quintessential radio horror host, combining a spooky persona with gallows humor, was Raymond Edward Johnson (sometimes referred to as simply "Raymond" or "Mr. Host") on *Inner Sanctum*, premiering on the Blue Network the year before *Suspense* and *The Whistler*. To the accompanying sound of a creaking door (the only sound effect, when the show was airing, to be granted a copyright by the Library of Congress), radio actor and announcer Raymond introduced myriad strange stories, some of them outright horror, others offbeat tales of crime and mystery. Some of *Inner Sanctum's* dramas starred horror icon Boris Karloff.

Here is a typical Raymond opening, his introduction to the drama "Till Death Do Us Part" (October 27, 1942):

> Good evening, friends of the *Inner Sanctum*. This is your host, bidding you welcome to the squeaking door. We're having a class reunion here tonight. Perhaps you'd like to meet some of our alumni. Oh, yes, everyone here has a degree ... third degree to be exact.
>
> You see that fellow over there riding the hobby horse ... with his head stuck under his arm? Well, he was decapitated on an *Inner Sanctum* play a few weeks ago. Now he's auditioning ... for the part of the Headless Horseman. [*fiendish laughter*] Or that little chap over there, the lonesome-looking fellow.... He's a pickpocket. Yeah, poor chap. Whenever he gets real lonely he goes out in the crowd for a little change [*chuckles eerily*].
>
> By the way, have you heard our class yell? It's just one word: Ouch! And our school colors ... black and blue, of course [more laughter].

Raymond also commented on the stories during the commercial break and after their climax, spicing his narration with a barrage of ghoulish jokes and puns. Each *Inner Sanctum* radio broadcast ended with Raymond, to the sound of that creaking door closing, bidding his listeners, "Pleasant ... dreams, hmmmmmmm...?"

It is not unlikely that many of the later TV horror hosts or the scribes writing their lines had been listeners of *Inner Sanctum*.

There were *Inner Sanctum* spin-offs. The program would be the basis of a series of six low-budget, more subtle psychological horror movies made by Universal Pictures from 1943 to 1945. Five of them opened with the same prologue warning of potential murder, spoken in a library by a disembodied head (played by character actor David Hoffman) suspended inside a crystal ball. Five of the Lon Chaney Jr.–staring titles in this series — *Calling Dr. Death* (1943), *Weird Woman, Dead Man's Eyes* (both 1944), *The Frozen Ghost* and *Pillow of Death* (both 1945) — would become part of Screen Gems' *Shock!* package.

Later came two movies entitled *Inner Sanctum*. The first, made by M.R.S. in 1948, was "inspired" by the radio series, but no creepy character introduced the story. In 1991, independent director Fred Olen Ray made a horror movie titled *Inner Sanctum*, which had neither a host character nor connection with the radio series.

In 1954 a drastically toned-down version of *Inner Sanctum*— presenting fairly ordinary tales of mystery, crime and murder now, no actual horror — was syndicated to local television stations across the United States, with Paul McGrath serving as unseen host and narrator. Interestingly, reruns of this series were telecast in Chicago on Saturday nights in 1957, right after *Shock Theatre* ended, on a different channel.

Of all the hosts to introduce horror and mystery stories on radio, Raymond Edward Johnson was the most influential on future horror hosts, regardless of the medium in which they appeared.

Four-Color Horror Hosts

In the pre–*Shock Theatre* 1950s, Raymond Edward Johnson's style of introducing, interrupting (at commercial breaks) and then winding up the *Inner Sanctum* dramas, always with humor mixed with the horror, carried over directly to the medium of comic books.

Horror comic books, printed in four colors on cheap paper, often graphically depicting the most gruesome of horrors, were a phenomenon from 1950 through 1954. Many of these publications featured weird, supernatural and even monstrous host characters — *e.g., The Hand of Fate* (narrated either by Fate or Death), *Mister Mystery* and *This Magazine Is Haunted* (Dr. Death). Sometimes the hosts were ghosts, skeletons, mummies or simply mysterious humans that, like Raymond on *Inner Sanctum*, used outrageous puns and other forms of humor to introduce and then close the illustrated stories.

Most successful and popular of all comic book host characters, and those having a direct link to their radio precursors, were the three so-called "GhouLunatics" offered by publisher William M. Gaines' EC comic book line: the Old Witch, appearing primarily in her own book *The Haunt of Fear*, the Crypt Keeper, host of *Tales from the Crypt*, and the Vault Keeper, mostly featured in *The Vault of Horror*. (All three characters also told stories, most of them scripted by editor Al Feldstein, in each other's books.) A long-time fan of both the horror genre and radio drama, Bill Gaines based his Old Witch on the character he'd heard so often on the radio program *The Witch's Tale*.

Gaines' Old Witch occupied her own spot, called "The Witch's Cauldron," in her fellow "GhouLunatic," the Vault Keeper's, magazine. The hag's opening words in the last story, published in the last issue (40, cover dated January 1955) of *The Vault of Horror*, was the standard type of jargon spoken each issue by the three narrators (and also predicted the verbal style that would become typical of so many future horror hosts on TV):

> Hee, hee! So you've finally reached the HAUNT OF FEAR, eh? Well, hop right into my humble hut, 'cause I've really got a hunk of GUNK boiling for you in that CRAZY CAULDRON of mine! MmmmmBoy! That stench? Oh, that FUMIGATOR was here ... seems there were some FLEAS left over from V.K.'S putrid piece about the pooches! HEE! Anyhow, peoples, this delicious ditty took SIX DEGEN-ERATIONS of the FAMOUS FRANKENSTEIN FAMILY to develop, so let's have a bit of quiet while I open my big black book to the chapter on BLOBS and commence with the wretched story, as told to Dr. Emil Frankenstein himself, called ... ASHES TO ASHES!

Tales from the Crypt and *Vault of Horror* were adapted, in 1972 and 1973, respectively, to anthology horror films format by Amicus Productions in England. Only the first of these featured a host; but that movie's Crypt Keeper was a stoic, humorless character, played by the well-respected British actor Sir Ralph Richardson.

The Crypt Keeper would fare better on the small screen. In 1989, *Tales from the Crypt*, with updated adaptations of the original horror comics stories (also some from EC's *Crime SuspensStories* and *Shock SuspensStories* comic books), would also transfer over to television, becoming an extremely popular cable TV series on the HBO cable channel. The Crypt Keeper was a puppet created and animated by movie special-effects artist Kevin Yagher and was voiced by actor John Kassir. In this incarnation the Crypt Keeper was por-trayed as a hysterically cackling, zombie-like character.

She Was a Vamp

The first TV personality who may be referred to as a horror host was the spooky "floating head" narrator played by radio personality Frank Gallop on *Lights Out*, a TV series that began in 1950, based on the popular and earlier radio series of the same name. Speaking in his deep voice and twisting his facial features, Gallop — who had, in a slightly related vein, provided narration for Paramount Pictures' "Casper the Friendly Ghost" animated cartoons — presented an imposing figure as he introduced, then gave final comments on, the series' stories of horror and the supernatural.

But *Lights Out* was a network show broadcast on NBC. What the author considers a horror host, in the *Shock Theatre* tradition anyway, is a character seen on local rather than network television channels.

Among the earliest local TV horror hosts, predating even pioneers in the genre like John Zacherle, was Maila Nurmi who, one night in 1954 on Los Angeles station KABC-7, made her debut appearance as the very sexy star of *The Vampira Show*. Vampira would make her appearance wearing a long black, form-fitting gown, sauntering down a candlelit corridor draped in cobwebs and filled with mist. Getting closer to the camera, she resembled the classic image of a female vampire — pale skin, high-arching eyebrows, long black hair, all weird yet incredibly appealing.

Finally up close, she would shriek, then say to her home audience, "Good evening. I am Vampira."

Vampira was ahead of her time in more than one way. Movies of any kind were still relatively rare on television when Nurmi was doing her video act, and most of the films that were available to local stations tended to come from "Poverty Row," most of them cheap Westerns. Among the pictures shown on *The Vampira Show* were such creaky cheapies as *Revenge of the Zombies* (1943), *The Flying Serpent* (1946) and *Devil Bat's Daughter* (1946).

Beyond her Vampira television performances (one of which found her acting opposite Bela Lugosi in a comedy skit on the variety program *The Milton Burle Show* (NBC), Nurmi also had a brief motion picture career. Her best known credit — largely because director Tim Burton immortalized it in his 1994 biopic movie *Ed Wood*— was in Wood's infamous *Plan 9 from Outer Space* (1959) wherein she played a walking corpse that looked, albeit with a more plunging neckline, exactly like Vampira.

Vampira is often credited as local television's first horror host (or, more accurately in her case, hostess). Her original show did run on Los Angeles television three years before any such hosts were introducing Screen Gems' *Shock!* package. But there was one local character who had already been on television,

The very popular Vampira (Maila Nurmi), of *The Vampira Show*, spiced her introductions of old low-budget horror and mystery films with sex appeal. Her show premiered on Los Angeles local station KABC-TV, Channel 7, in 1954 (courtesy John Skerchock).

showing horror movies and scaring his viewers, several years before Vampira ever slinked her way down that misty corridor.

Like Marvin, this character and his show originated from Chicago.

Chicago TV's First Horror Host

From as early as January of 1951 through late 1953, the sinister swami Drana Badour introduced horror and mystery movies on the WBKB (then still Channel 4) late-night program *Murder Before Midnight*. The show was so-called because, unlike radio's similarly titled *Murder at Midnight* mystery series, the swami's program aired at 10:45 PM, before the official witching hour.

Unlike what was the norm for *The Vampira Show* and the later *Shock Theatre*, *Murder Before Midnight* did not run one complete movie per night. Instead, perhaps because of the dearth of genre titles available back in 1951, the program broke each film up into three segments, serial-style, spreading a single movie across three consecutive nights. Even more amazing, *Murder Before Midnight* did not air on a once-per-week basis. Also unusual, the show, rather than being on a strictly weekday schedule, was telecast six nights every week (Monday through Saturday).

Drana Badour was originally played by WBKB announcer Allen Harvey. Dressed in full Arabian garb, Harvey sat on a rug gesturing mystically over a crystal ball, at the same time speaking lines that had the power to scare some viewers of early television, especially the younger members of the audience allowed to stay up late enough to watch the show.

As the camera pushed in closer on the swami's crystal ball he would introduce that night's film (or segment of it). The film would first show inside the crystal ball, then, as the globe faded away, commence on its own. Some of them were merely old who-dunits and crime thrillers, including titles from

Monogram's Charlie Chan series (e.g., *Dark Alibi, Shadow Over Chinatown* and *The Red Dragon*), all of them low-budget productions starring Sidney Toler. Some of the swami's films were actual (or at least borderline) horror thrillers, such as *White Zombie* (1932), *The Corpse Vanishes* (1942) and *The Ape Man* (1943), all starring Bela Lugosi, *Return of the Ape Man* (1944), with Lugosi and John Carradine, *The Thirteenth Guest* (1932), *Terror House* (1942) and, again with Carradine, *The Face of Marble* (1946).

Drana Badour would interrupt the movie to telephone someone presumably at home watching, offering a prize (furnished by the show's sponsor, local automobile dealership Allied Motors) if the person at the

Chicago television's first horror host was the spooky swami Drana Badour (Allen Harvey), who introduced horror and mystery movies on *Murder Before Midnight* telecast on the original WBKB (Channel 4). The show began running in 1951 and aired six nights per week, spreading each film over several days. The swami also quizzed viewers over the telephone and awarded prizes.

other end of the line could correctly answer the swami's question relating to the plot of that night's movie.

By 1953, following the acquisition of the original WBKB by CBS, *Murder Before Midnight,* was airing on WBBM (Channel 2). The program now ran on a more traditional Monday through Friday schedule, showing one movie in *two* nights.

Not only had the program's schedule changed, but so had Drana Badour. Harvey was replaced as the swami by Art Hern, who was just beginning his long-time association with Chicago television. Hern was already a seasoned radio performer by the time he donned the Swami's robes and turban. His audio credits included, for a while, playing the continuing role of Ichabod "Ikky" Mudd on the popular children's adventure serial *Captain Midnight.* Making the transition from radio to Chicago television, Hern, wearing various makeups and costumes, endeared himself to a generation of young Chicagoans playing such characters as the second Natco the Clown on *Adventure Time* (Natco introducing 1930s movie serials like *Flash Gordon, Mystery Squadron* and *The Hurricane Express*), first mate Moby on *The Happy Pirates* and the lead character on *The Pied Piper.*

Coincidentally, on *Adventure Time,* Hern also did a telephone segment wherein he asked questions of viewers hoping to win a prize; and on *The Happy Pirates,* he played opposite singer–piano player Dick "Two Ton" Baker, Squawky the parrot and Bubbles the porpoise, the latter a puppet made by Bruce Newton, the future Frankenstein Monster character on *Shock Theatre.*

Four years after his stint as the host of *Murder Before Midnight,* Hern would play a minor yet monstrous role in *Shock Theatre*'s earliest history.

As *The Wolf Man* winds down and fades out, Marvin is applying a blowtorch to Dear's feet, the more grisly consequences of his latest shenanigans tastefully kept in shadow.

"She always complains about cold feet," he explains. "Well, that was our story for tonight. Wasn't it enjoyable? I should mention that the characters in tonight's play, unfortunately, were real. Next week's story, we thought you'd like to know ... will not give you nightmares. That's because you probably won't be able to fall asleep. Shall we see a little of it?"

The TV image briefly switches to a "coming attractions" trailer for *Night Monster,* starring Bela Lugosi.

"We'll expect to see you boys and ghouls here then! And, oh, I would like to thank you for your wonderful letters. Naturally, they were poison pen letters ... and we took them from the dead letter box. Many of you requested pictures. Unfortunately, we've sealed our photographer in the darkroom."

Marvin picks up a little doll and a handful of pins.

"And now it's time for us to say good night. Say good night." Gleefully he sticks some of the pins in the doll.

Naturally Dear screams.
"Have a horrible week!"

Its third week on the air, December 21, 1957, *Shock Theatre* gave viewers their Christmas present: *Night Monster*, a 1942 horror movie in which "star" Bela Lugosi had a "red herring" role as a butler. The "night monster" of the title was actually just a murderous, legless old man, played by Ralph Morgan, who materializes a pair of hairy limbs by sheer will power.

"Well, we've got a nifty story for you tonight," Marvin says, introducing the film's opening segment. "And this is not the life story of [local Chicago TV personality] Marty Faye. The Night Monster is horrible, it's *vicious* ... frightening ... it's *ugly*. In other words, it's my idea of a comedy."

The next week, the last Saturday night of December, Marvin gave *Shock Theatre* fans something more in the line of a real "monster."

3

Beginning Shock Treatment

On December 28, 1957, viewers living in Chicago and its suburbs were again drawn into the weird yet wonderful world of *Shock Theatre* and its maniacal host character, in real life the very talented and versatile Terry Bennett

"Good evening. I'm Marvin. Tonight's story is *The Mummy.*

"A mummy is very similar to a skeleton. And as you know, a skeleton is a man with his insides out and his outsides ... off. *The Mummy* is the story of a man who went to buy a suit from one of those places with no overhead and came out wearing one of the racks. Our story takes place in Egypt, which accounts for the fact that our hero has a great stone face. Boris Karloff plays the part of the Mummy with such realism that already he's received fan mail from three pieces of cheesecloth. There's one nice thing about being a mummy. You never have to dress to go out. Although I know one mummy who was so successful he had three changes of rags."

Following a commercial, on this last show of 1957, Marvin returns.

"And now for the story of *The Mummy*, taken from the hit song 'Does Your Mummy Come from Ireland.' Our story takes place in Egypt, and you may see a lot of romantic old ruins. Most of them, however, are married. The story of *The Mummy* proves that we all come from the same mold. However, the Mummy is moldier than most of us. But now our story..."

In the opening shot of *The Mummy*, we see the Scroll of Thoth. "This is not a parking ticket," explains Marvin in a voice-over. "It's merely an excerpt from the magazine *Ancient Romance*, the magazine for teenage mummies."

Morty Goldman, "Vent"

Morton Goldman — the future Terry Bennett — was born in Brooklyn, New York, on April 25, 1930.

Morty (as his family and friends usually called him) was a talented, creative and sensitive child. He was also ambitious and enterprising. At the age of nine he was already employed, working at Goldberg's Delicatessen, getting paid $12 per week plus all the frankfurters he could eat. Morty had bigger dreams and so, when this job lasted only two months, he did not consider it any major loss. When he was working at Goldberg's, his thoughts often drifted toward what was then his maid ambition: becoming a professional magician.

When Morty wasn't working he would occasionally rush off to the Mayfair Theatre to catch the latest vaudeville shows. It was during these shows that the boy saw his first in-person ventriloquist acts. As he would later recall in his uncompleted autobiography:

I don't recall [the ventriloquist's] name, but he was darn good! I laughed, and thrilled, and laughed, and thrilled! He was truly a marvelous venTHRILLOquist.

It was then that I decided there were too many magicians, and not enough ventriloquists.

There was no advertisement for *Night Monster* in the *TV Guide* for the week that movie played on *Shock Theatre*, perhaps because the film had no real monster, *Night* or otherwise. But the next issue featured a full-page ad for the program's fourth movie *The Mummy*—although the creature feature is actually Lon Chaney, Jr. from *The Mummy's Curse*.

How was I to get a ventriloquial figure? My chum Burt Lipshitz solved that problem better than John J. Anthony. *He* was my dummy. I'd pull a lock of his hair, and he would open his mouth. But good old Burt, sometimes it was so hard for him to shut his mouth. Hard, it was practically impossible.

For the boy's tenth birthday, Morty's Uncle Irving gave him a dummy in the image of Edgar Bergen's Charlie McCarthy of radio and motion picture

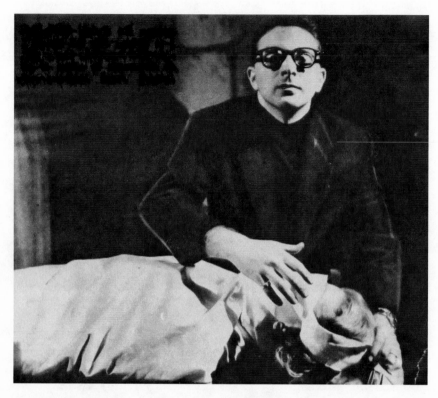

Marvin (Terry Bennett) wraps and will stamp Dear (Dorothy Johnson) for shipping during a *Shock Theatre* break in *The Mummy*.

fame. By now Morty's friend Burt was demanding payment for his dummy act, so the Charlie figure could not have arrived at a more opportune time.

One day, Morty, then of junior high school age, happened to be listening to John J. Anthony's popular radio program *The Good Will Hour*, a show that allowed people to voice their problems on the air hoping that some listener might come to the rescue with a solution. Writing to Anthony and wrangling a spot on the show, Morty, accompanied by his supportive mother, pleaded his case into the studio microphone:

> We came home from the broadcast quite late that evening, and when we reached home, we were swamped with phone calls from relatives and friends who told me that I sounded great on the air. The broadcast had served its purpose in more ways than one.
>
> Next day, I received an envelope with additional letters from people who wanted to help me. Among these was a circular from FRANK MARSHALL, the leading figure maker of the century.
>
> He had a small ten-inch figure for sale, a sailor, cost — ten dollars!

I sent for it! When I received it, I played with it all day, like a girl with a doll. Come to think of it, I wish I was playing with the girl all day, and let the dummy play with the doll.

Anyway, the figure was still too small for professional engagements. But, I thought, I could try an act in school.

Dubbing the new figure Timothy Timber (a name he would retain for future professional use), Morty, at the suggestion of a teacher, performed the following week for fellow students in his junior high school auditorium. He was a hit and became known to almost everyone in his school

After much practice with the McCarthy and Marshall figures, 14-year-old Morty was already an accomplished ventriloquist. During those formative years, the youth continued to develop his ventriloquist's abilities and techniques, and also to perfect the voice and define the character of his dummy. Morty's audience during those early years consisted mainly of his friends and relatives. But that limited group would soon expand.

Around that time the boy purchased, from the famous Lou Tannen's Magic Store in New York City, a couple of the standard-issue ventriloquist dummies made by John C. Turner. They were the kinds of figures that were used by most practitioners of the art since the 1940s. Morty's career as a professional ventriloquist was beginning. With the Turner dummy (which Terry named Red Flannels) in tow, he entered talent contests (winning many of

High school student Morton Goldman (later Terry Bennett) and his first Red Flannels dummy (or, more correctly, figure), here posed with popular radio and recording personality Arthur Godfrey. "Morty" appeared on Godfrey's radio show the day this photograph was snapped (courtesy Kerry Bennett).

them), performed on weekends at the RKO and Loew's Theaters in New York, and, joining a young but talented group of semi-professionals, went on a USO tour to entertain the military.

While attending Abraham Lincoln High School in Brooklyn, Morty returned to radio, but this time not to get a problem solved. Winning an audition, the teenager soon found himself in the CBS studios doing his act on Arthur Godfrey's immensely popular morning program. The performance went well and new doors of opportunity began to open for Morty.

By the time Morty was 17 years old, he was a well-known New York personality, approached by local agents who began to offer him professional work. The teenage ventriloquist was soon appearing on the then still young medium of television on programs hosted by such celebrities as Johnny Johnston and Kate Smith. This TV exposure led to bigger and more lucrative gigs in theaters and nightclubs, where Morty appeared with top-name headliners in such major cities as New York, Miami, Washington, D.C. and New Orleans.

Morty also got to meet one of his heroes:

When I was still attending Abraham Lincoln High School, I had the honor and privilege of meeting Edgar Bergen, the world-famous ventriloquist ... [He] was playing an engagement at the Waldorf Astoria [Hotel] in New York.... I arrived at the Waldorf Astoria about ten in the morning, preparing for the eleven o'clock appointment. Mr. Bergen had given me fifteen minutes of his time.

At eleven o'clock, I reached the suite, and

A professional "head shot" of young Terry Bennett with his first Red Flannels, purchased through the mail from Lou Tannen's Magic Store in New York City. The dummy (or figure) was "standard issue," made by John C. Turner and used by many amateur and professional ventriloquists during the 1940s (courtesy Kerry Bennett).

after wiping my hands of the perspiration, I knocked quite uneasily. A young lady answered, and I was ushered in. Mr. Bergen entered, and we were formally introduced. He asked me about myself, and also asked me to do my act. I did, and the thought of Mr. Bergen sitting opposite me, with legs crossed and his head in his hands, leaves me with chills.

I finished my act with the dummy in the suitcase. At last, Mr. Bergen laughed. He showed me Charlie McCarthy, and took my name and address. When I left, I realized that we had been together for almost an hour. I left the Waldorf, with my head in the clouds....

... But I was taught a lesson from my meeting with Edgar Bergen. No matter how big a person gets, it's nice to remember the little fellow on the way up. To this day I have the deepest respect and admiration for Mr. Bergen, not only as the world's greatest ventriloquist, but for being the "regular'" fellow that he is.

Our little meeting shall always remain a pleasant inspiration for me.

The money Morty earned by performing allowed him to realize a dream he had since first learning how to make an inanimate object talk to have his own *original* figure. That meant that the young ventriloquist had to go to Chicago and finally meet the country's foremost creator of ventriloquist dummies, a true master of his craft. For a "vent" to own an original Frank Marshall creation meant that he or she had "made it" or was about to "make it."

Morty described for Marshall the kind of figure that he wanted for his act, then the teenager waited as Marshall went to work. Morty planned to name it Red Flannels. Three months later Marshall presented the finished and very appealing Red Flannels to the young ventriloquist, establishing a strong and enduring friendship between them.

Joy Joins the Act

She was a beautiful young woman who stood about five feet four inches tall (although newspaper and magazine articles would later describe her as "statuesque").

Joy Ann Page, born in Milwaukee, Wisconsin, was a promising ballerina when she and her mother moved to Florida. On the evening of August 4, 1950, in Tampa, Joy and her mother went to a combination nightclub and dinner club located on the top floor of the Bay Shore Royal Hotel (now the Bay Shore Royal Condo). Joy happened to notice the elevator opening on that floor, and out of it stepped a strapping young man. The man, Joy would learn, was a ventriloquist who had been touring the country with his act. This night, a fateful one as it would turn out, he was to perform at the hotel nightclub.

Kerry Bennett described the event as related to him by his mother Joy:

Apparently when the door opened up, my dad stepped off the elevator, did a 360-degree "spin" and, at the end of that spin, put out his cigarette in one of those floor-standing ashtrays. So it was like a flamboyant way of putting out his cigarette and making a grand entrance.

Later that night, Terry told Joy's mom, "One day I'm going to marry your daughter."

That "one day" was not immediate in coming.

Morty's career with Red Flannels, as well as his dating Joy (and keeping the promise he'd made to her mom), abruptly halted in the spring of 1951, courtesy of Uncle Sam. Drafted into the United States Army, Morty was shipped off to Orleans, France. Accompanying him overseas was his wooden friend and partner Red Flannels. The team of Morty and Red entertained the troops for the duration of his two-year stint. On September 3 of that year, for example, Private Morty Goldman, then a member of the Service Battery, 34th FA Battalion, won the post-wide talent contest finals held at his base's sports arena.

Morty's discharge from the Army in 1953 was not without minor fanfare involving Red Flannels. A base newspaper clipping, headlined "Flannels' Farewell" and accompanied by an "Army Photo" of Red seated at a typewriter, stated the following:

> Red Flannels, ventriloquist dummy belonging to Sgt. Morton Goldman, of the Com Z Special Activities Division, types out his last column for the command's newspaper, the *Com Z Cadence*. A featured columnist for the past 18 months, Flannels is returning to the U.S. with Goldman to enter show business.

Upon returning from Europe, Morton Goldman, now 23 years old, found himself in the position many performers do after being away from the entertainment industry for any considerable length of time: He was unemployed. His former business contacts were gone and he basically had to start his career over again. Fortunately Morty happened to be a go-getter. He had drive as well as talent and good looks and the time had come to move forward.

One of the first things Morty did was to change his name legally to Terry Bennett. It was also time for the newly renamed ventriloquist to create a new act, one that would include a recent addition to his personal life: At last honoring his word to Joy's mother, Terry reconnected with the beauty, then only 18 years old. On June 18, 1953, Terry and Joy married.

A talented performer herself, Joy wanted to be more than just Terry's wife; Se wanted to become an active part of her husband's ventriloquist act. Soon the team was on a tour in Canada that lasted for about a year. The tour afforded the couple the time needed to perfect their act.

Terry Bennett and pre-blonde Joy Ann Page enjoy a night out on the town. Photograph courtesy Kerry Bennett.

Upon completing their Canadian tour, the Bennetts decided to officially start their new career in the city of Red Flannels' "birth," Chicago.

In 1954, Terry's "big break" seemed to arrive. He was hired that year by Chicago television station WBKB-TV where he had many creative hats, most of them worn behind the cameras. Terry soon found himself busy writing, devising advertisement campaigns, designing logos (including the station's) and performing whatever other duties he was called upon by the upper brass to execute.

Yet, despite his being so active at an actual television station, Terry was not entirely satisfied with his myriad assignments. He was a performer — and none of the jobs he was doing at Channel 7 were taking advantage of his abilities, especially his skills as a ventriloquist.

Thus, following two years of such work, Terry considered moving over to another local television station, WGN (Channel 9). As reported in a newspaper clipping dated January 20, 1956:

> Over at WGN-TV programming boss Jay Faraghan agreed to interview a ventriloquist named Terry Bennett. Terry stalked in with his dummy unlimbered for conversation. Dummy took one glassy-eyed look at Faraghan's Ronald Colman–type mustache and blurted, "Say, is that a mustache or did he swallow a cat?" Jay says for the first time in 20 kilocycle years, he couldn't think of a thing to say.

Whether or not Faraghan was truly amused by Red Flannels' quip, Terry did not get hired by WGN.

But his career opportunities were beginning to improve over at WBKB. That same year Terry and Joy, along with Red Flannels, were finally awarded their own half-hour program, *Flannel Land, U.S.A.*, telecast live at 9:30 Sunday mornings. The show was sponsored by Polk Bros., the Midwest's largest carpeting, furniture and appliance retail chain. Terry already had history with Polk Bros.: from 1952 to 1954 Terry had been the writer and media supervisor for the stores.

An August 8, 1956, newspaper item described how Terry and company were now helping move products sold by Polk Bros.:

> Polk Bros. is using a half-hour ventriloquist show for children every Saturday [*sic*] to move its products.
> Terry Bennett and his dummy, Red Flannels, "ham it up" for a total of six minutes of commercials each program, pointing out the top features of TV, freezers, etc.
> This weekend, Mr. Bennett, his wife, Joy, who aids as a story teller, and the dummy pushed a Super 200 chassis Admiral TV console set at $199.95, plus Admiral refrigerator-freezer. A complete zoo of stuffed animals, valued by Polk's $44.80, was offered with the refrigerator-freezer in a combination package for $394.95....

... Children up to 13 years of age will be asked to send in their sketches of Red Flannels, and Mr. Bennett, his wife and staff will serve as judges. They plan to present the winner on the air.

The Mummy ends, just moments after its title character crumbles to dust and a pile of ancient bandages.

"And that was our story for tonight," says Marvin on this fourth night of *Shock Theatre*. "Wasn't it delightful? I just love musicals, don't you? I asked the Mummy to come out for an encore ... but he just can't pull himself together. He's so emotional.

"Next week we have a cartoon that's just hilarious. Some friends of mine saw it and they just died laughing. What a wonderful way to go. We'll see a little of it after the poem for the day, sent in by one of our fiends....

"Marvin poisoned his father's tea,

"Father died in agony.

"Mother came and looked quite vexed....

"Really, Mar, she said, what's next?

"And now for our preview...."

Following a trailer for next week's movie *Murders in the Rue Morgue* starring Bela Lugosi, Marvin says, "And now it's time for us to go. Say goodnight, Dear."

Dear, her mouth off camera, produces the sound of a siren rather than a scream.

"Say, her voice is changing."

Marvin also wished viewers a "Happy New Year," ending the last show of 1957.

4

Pre-Shock Anticipation

Shock Theatre began its first show of 1958 as it had for the past three weeks. Following that now familiar opening, Marvin descended the cellar stairs and addressed his audience:

"Hello, I'm Marvin. Judging from your letters, we've had a lot of requests, but I'm back anyway. Well, I made a New Year's resolution not to twist her neck, but I broke it. The neck, not the resolution. I never break those."

For a moment, he reminisces.

"We had a wonderful New Year's. We went to the Monster's house to celebrate. It's a little difficult to find. You have to go down six feet. It's like a garden apartment with real gardens. You should see the place. The faucets have hot and cold running poison for people who like their poison warmed. That cold stuff gives you the shivers. Dracula came to the party and, of course, he brought his own drinks. The Wolf Man was there, too, but he stayed until the moon came out, and then he had a call to make. What a party! You might say it was a sick house ... and if you got a sick house, I know a guy in Oklahoma named [singer] Sam Speed ... and this guy..."

After a commercial, as Dear is taking down a Christmas tree:

"Now, our story tonight is *Murders in the Rue Morgue* ... the story of a man who committed a murder and got a suspended sentence. He was hung. Imagine, he killed a little old woman for just three dollars. But three dollars here, three dollars there, it all adds up. Most of our story takes place in a morgue, where guests are uninvited, but still manage to stay a long time. Yes, there are a lot of murders in tonight's story, and you'll find there are very few clues as to the whereabouts of the police. The story you are about to see is true. Nothing has been changed except the police ... to protect the public.

"Where do you think our story starts? In a morgue? A circus? A TV studio? No, it starts like this..."

Murders in the Rue Morgue opens with a scene of a boat cruising down the river Seine. The motion picture was Universal's 1932 adaptation of Edgar Allan Poe's classic story, regarded by literary scholars as the first detective story. The movie told the lurid tale of mad Dr. Mirakle (Bela Lugosi), a sci-

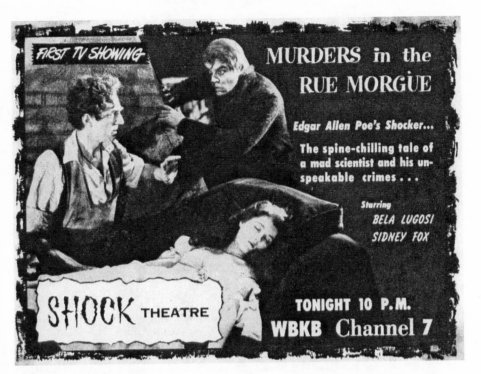

TV Guide advertisement for the fifth movie shown on *Shock Theatre*, this one not given the full-page treatment.

entist trying to prove Darwin's theory of evolution by mixing the blood of women with that of a huge killer ape. As would be expected, all Mirakle proves is that when one dabbles in mad science, only disaster and horror result.

The first break in the movie ended with a scene of Dr. Mirakle outside in the fog stalking towards two men, both armed with swords, dueling to the death over a streetwalker (played by Arlene Francis, an actress who would, two decades later, become famous as a panelist on the popular TV and radio quiz show *What's My Line?*).

As made-up by Universal's resident wizard Jack Pierce, Lugosi, moving into the scene, cuts a striking image, particularly with the fake thick black eyebrows that Pierce had applied.

Marvin, holding a sword, is standing close to Dear
"Here comes our hero," observes Marvin. "He just wants to see if those men are fixed for blades."
Marvin brandishes his sword.
"Oh, I'm just teaching Her how to duel. But, isn't Dr. Mirakle cute? See his

eyebrows? He puts them up in curlers every night. They're good-looking eyebrows. They must be. He's already received three love letters from Elvis Presley's sideburns."

Marvin's attention goes to the weapon and then to the woman..

"Oh, excuse me a moment. I've got to teach Her how to duel. Don't be afraid: Just do as I do. Now, when I lunge..."

He lunges ... and Dear moans, then drops.

"Get off the floor! This is no time to take a nap. I'm teaching you how to duel. *En garde...!*

Shock Theatre! *Comes to Chicago*

For a total, thus far, of four consecutive weeks, Marvin had been killing or at least torturing his very resilient young woman accomplice. Each fiendish act — and nearly every aspect of *Shock Theatre*— was the brainchild of Terry Bennett.

Yet without the decision of one particular executive at WBKB, perhaps the program might never have started up in Chicago. Before anyone could even think about a show called *Shock Theatre*, someone in power at the station

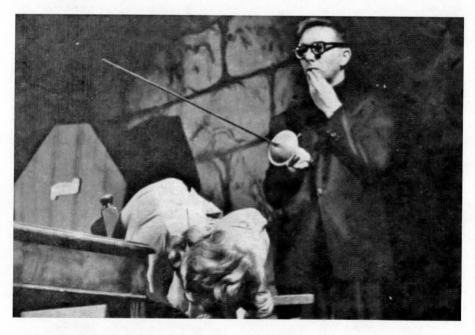

On the night *Shock Theatre* ran *Murders in the Rue Morgue*, Marvin (Terry Bennett) tried demonstrating to Dear (Dorothy Johnson) the fine art of fencing — with unsurprising results.

needed to purchase Screen Gems' package of 52 movies. Fortunately for fans of horror movies, WBKB had just such a person.

So far those *Shock!* motion pictures were hiking up television ratings in whatever city they played. Their success in New York, Philadelphia, San Antonio, Los Angeles and San Francisco was noted by WBKB's upper brass, especially program director Sterling C. Quinlan.

"Red" Quinlan, so nicknamed, not surprisingly, because of his bright blond-red hair, began his media career as a columnist for *The Southend Reporter* and as a broadcaster describing his travels Out West on Chicago radio station WMAQ. He got his start at the original WBKB as a crew member, but gradually worked his way up the station's hierarchy ladder until securing an executive position. During his years at WBKB, from its early days as Channel 4, then continuing through its time as a CBS affiliate, and finally in its later incarnation as Channel 7, Quinlan evolved the station into what would become local powerhouse WLS-TV. He would be instrumental in boosting the professional careers of local talk show host Lee Phillip Bell, comedian Bob Newhart and news anchor Frank Reynolds. Indeed, Quinlan became well known for his willingness to give chances to new talent and to test new ideas when it came to programming.

Taking note of the commercial possibilities of Screen Gems' *Shock!* package, Quinlan, along with Matt Veracker, another WBKB employee, purchased the 52 movies for his station.

Terry Bennett, at the time, was still primarily a behind-the-cameras Channel 7 employee and serving many functions that included creating the on-air logo for the ABC network and doing on-air promotions for such network shows as *The Ford Hour,* starring Tennessee Ernie Ford, and *Maverick,* which debuted less than three months before *Shock Theatre* had its first airing. Knowing that Quinlan had acquired the Screen Gems package, Bennett immediately saw its potential and approached the general manager and program director Dan Schuffman with his creative ideas ... and he had many of them ... for showcasing the movies.

As Joy Bennett told interviewer Rick Thomas in his 2004 article about *Shock Theatre,* published in *Filmfax* magazine, "My husband was, and had always been, a ventriloquist — he simply conceived the idea of what could be done with the *Shock Theater* package, and then convinced Red Quinlan that we could probably pull it off."

On the morning of November 11, 1957, on a page of the *Chicago Sun-Times,* the column "It's the Malloy," written daily by television critic Paul Malloy, opened with an intriguing headline: "WBKB To Do Its Scary Best to Shock You."

It was hardly a secret to readers of the column that Malloy was no big fan of the horror genre in whatever medium it appeared. Indeed, Malloy often railed against such films and television shows, particularly those showing violence. "If you've felt insecure lately — relax," he began his piece. "Strange things are happening and we're all off balance."

Following some light Chicago-related patter, including a comment about local celebrity Marty Faye helping his "little old lady" mother across State Street, Malloy went on to reveal the following:

> Station WBKB (Channel 7) has acquired the 52-film package of horror movies which has been racking up almost incredible ratings in New York, Los Angeles and Philadelphia. They will be shown Saturday nights at 10 P.M., long after children and timid adults have gone beddyby. The march of the monsters leads off Dec. 7, something of a day of infamy to begin with. Pacing the pack of monsters will be Boris Karloff in *Frankenstein*, granddaddy of the great undead.

Chicagoans who loved the movies starring the likes of Frankenstein's Monster and Count Dracula, and missed seeing such films again and again in local movie houses once Realart's deal with Universal-International ended, must have reacted for at least a few moments in stunned silence. To date none of the Universal horror pictures (aside from some Sherlock Holmes titles with "horror" elements) had played on television. Could what Malloy had written be true? *Frankenstein*—the *original* movie with Boris Karloff— as well *51 other* horror movies, would, be showing and for free on the family television set?

But Malloy's words were in print and in a newspaper, so they must be true! And what about those other 51?

> All of Frankie's playmates, including "The Bride of Frankenstein," will be round on succeeding Saturdays. There'll be "Dracula," the Hungarian lush with a weakness for Bloody Marys; "Son of Dracula"; "Dracula's Daughter" and eventually, I suppose, "Dracula's Other Wife." Another series will be that of "The Mummy," followed by "The Mummy's Tomb," "The Mummy's Hand" and "The Mummy's Ghost." In time, no doubt, we can expect something current like "I Was a Teenage Mummy," which has nothing to do with unwed mothers.
>
> The package includes "The Werewolf of London" and "The Werewolf of Paris" [*sic*]. (No, Virginia, there is no "Werewolf of Disneyland"— yet.) It will showcase the grunt and groan talents of Bela Lugosi, Lon Chaney Jr., Basil Rathbone, Orson Welles [*sic*] and John Carradine in such quaint vignettes as "The Mad Ghoul," "House of Horrors" and, so help me, "The Spider Woman Strikes Back."

Malloy reported that Columbia Pictures was releasing this "grisly project" and that the success of this film package had already "startled the trade with the audience results.... "The televampires and their little friends boosted ratings anywhere from 38 to several hundred percent," thereby collapsing any and all competition running opposite the movies.

> ... The current *Life* magazine reports that horror movies, the new ones playing the theaters, are the biggest money makers as a group in the business. Why? I'd

say because Americans have reached a point of tension where they see little green men stumbling out of little pink saucers. They take tranquillizers only to find that the little men have turned pink, and the little saucers have turned green.

So they find temporary solace in the never-never land of monsters or in the stereotyped pattern of blazing sixguns and galloping hooves. For escapism, too, is behind the long-sustained lure of the Western.

The next trend is inevitable: Some smart producer will connect both themes into a single storyline, and we will have the horror Western. The next generation may look forward to such promising series as *Wyatt Hearse, Wild Bill Hickorpse* and *Have Shroud, Will Travel.*

Malloy did not, however, mention the name of the program that would show these 52 films; nor did he give even the slightest hint as to what WBKB, thanks to Terry Bennett's imaginative efforts to do something special, had in mind.

Agreeing with Terry's ideas, Channel 7 program director Dan Schuffman, on November 19, issued the following "American Broadcasting Company Interdepartment Correspondence" to WBKB staffers, finally revealing the new show's title:

> Beginning this week you will be visited during your show by some representatives of the Nether World. This week a gorilla, next week a mummy, the following week — well, by then we think you will really be in the fun of this promotion for *Shock Theater.*
>
> We're playing it for laughs, but for as much promotion as possible. *Shock Theater* begins December 7th, Saturday night at 10:00 PM. We will be going directly opposite *The Best of MGM* on CBS. And, with our lead off picture *Frankenstein* we think we can completely capture the "lion" share of the audience.
>
> If you can think about it for a moment, you'll realize that these pictures are a curiosity for most people. Those who have seen them will want to see them again just to check — were they as good or bad as they remember them? For new viewers, they mean excitement and suspense — tension relievers. For all viewers there will be a host or hostess on the show who will help give them an excuse to watch. Many people will be reluctant to admit they *want* to watch a Frankenstein movie, but they can always say "I just watched to see what the M.C. is going to do next." Thus goes the twisted humor of most of us.
>
> So, when you find a shrunken head on your show, or a skull — play it to the hilt for a good promotion for *Shock Theater* Saturday, December 7th at 10:00 P.M.
>
> All Directors please note: There will be live on-camera promos in station breaks and shows to be done by Terry Bennett. Check your schedule carefully and work with Terry to make these sharp, clean and effective.

Monsters Invade Downtown

To promote *Shock Theatre*, WBKB did what it often did when requiring props to be built or characters to be impersonated: It recruited people already on Channel 7's payroll for double, even *triple* duty.

For the job of publicizing the new program in a big and eye-catching way, WBKB brought into extra service three of its stalwart veterans, Bruce Newton, Ronny Born and the former second Drana Badour of *Murder Before Midnight* fame, Art Hern. Their new assignment was to impersonate monsters, indeed the very kinds of creatures that viewers would soon be watching each weekend in the *Shock Theatre* movies, *i.e.*, Frankenstein's Monster, a living mummy and, although really not a monster in the strict definition of the term, a gorilla.

A big (6' 4"), husky man and already a member of the WBKB staff, Bruce Newton was the perfect choice to be drafted into wearing a Frankenstein Monster guise for the new show's promotions. "I was hired by Red Quinlan after he became general manager," Newton told Rick Thomas in *Filmfax*. "We wore a lot of different hats."

Newton was also a designer and creator of props, an artist, sometimes script writer, occasional producer, even a puppeteer. He was born in Saginaw Bay, Michigan, and, following a stint in the United States Navy, he began his TV career as early as 1939, having been picked at random to be interviewed on the air about an exhibit on television. He entered Chicago TV after impressing various executives at WGN with the many things he could do.

In 1952, while employed by Channel 9, Newton designed, made and operated the puppet lead fowl on *Garfield Goose and Friend*, a children's program starring Frazier Thomas that would become a local TV classic. Around the time he created "Gar," as the goose was affectionately called, Newton was approached by Quinlan to join the staff at WBKB, the station then still airing over Channel 4 as part of the CBS network. Somewhat bitter over being denied a pay raise considering the extra work he was told to do on the *Garfield Goose* show, Newton accepted the offer.

"Red," Newton told Thomas, became a sort of mentor to him. Among Newton's assignments for Quinlan at his new workplace were creating the puppet Bubbles the porpoise on *The Happy Pirates*, a children program starring Dick "Two Ton" Baker and co-starring Art Hern, and various fanciful characters on *Princess Mary's Castle*, a kids' show starring former *Super Circus* bandleading majorette Mary Hartline. As Newton related to Thomas:

"We wore a lot of different hats. We would write bits, skits and commercials, find props, do visual work."

Newton didn't wear another of his myriad "hats" for his promotional stint as the Monster, but he did wear a mask.

The Treasure Chest, home of the Chicago Magic Center, was a great store for buying horror- and monster-related items in the late 1950s. Located on Randolph Street near State Street, the shop was conveniently within walk-

In the photo, handwritten text reads: To DON – from SHORTY (Bruce Newton)

Big Bruce Newton as the Frankenstein Monster promoting the upcoming *Shock Theatre* in the offices of WBKB-TV (courtesy Bruce Newton).

ing distance of the building in which WBKB had its studios. The store was a large one, more deep than wide. Basically a huge novelty shop, the Treasure Chest sold magic tricks, practical jokes, theatrical make-up, games and newspapers with gag headlines (printed up in the back of the store). It had a few booths where customers could make their own records and offered a variety of pinball and other penny arcade–type machines.

Ronny Born (mummy), Art Hern (gorilla) and Bruce Newton (Frankenstein's Monster) set out to promote *Shock Theatre* before the first show aired (courtesy Bruce Newton).

And the Treasure Chest sold masks — a wide variety of rubber face and over-the-head masks. There seemed to be a mask for any need and every occasion — caveman, wolf, gorilla, a couple varieties of skull, clown, a rotting corpse, cannibal, whatever. There was also a full head mask made in the image of the Frankenstein Monster.

In 1948, mask maker and movie prop builder Don Post struck a deal with Universal-International Pictures, coinciding with that company's release of the horror-comedy *Abbott and Costello Meet Frankenstein*, to design, manufacture and commercially sell rubber masks in the image of the Frankenstein Monster. The Frankenstein Monster mask that the Treasure Chest sold was one of Post's creations and was the most popular version sold during the 1950s. The face was green, the sculpted hair was black. There were red stitched scars (one on the right side of the forehead, the other on the left cheek) and silver forehead clamps neck electrodes. The mask generally sold over the counter for about $3.50 plus tax.

Newton walked over to the Treasure Chest and purchased this Frankenstein Monster mask. To help disguise the fact that the mask was entirely made of rubber, he glued stringy black artificial locks over the its sculpted and molded hair.

In addition to promoting *Shock Theatre* before it aired, Newton would be soon be called upon to do a variety of jobs on the show, mostly supplying props of a sinister or ghoulish nature. Whatever props he could not find, he either had to hope to find at the Treasure Chest or, if that failed, make them himself. And as *Shock Theatre* went into 1958, Newton would also become a regular cast member.

Ronny Born, like Newton and Art Hern, was a mainstay at Channel 7, mainly doing voice-over work on many programs. Basically a voice actor, Born supplied many of the words spoken for the characters, like an elf named Windy Widgett, created by Newton for *Princess Mary's Castle*. He also co-created the bizarre WBKB series *Chatter's World*. Chatter was an unpredictable, too often unruly chimpanzee who "talked," at least in a voice-over, and Born supplied Chatter's voice.

Like Newton, Born would, in less than a year, become another cast member of *Shock Theatre*.

The Frankenstein Monster, a nicely dressed gorilla and a living mummy, impersonated by Bruce Newton, Art Hern and Ronny Born, respectively, were ready to go into scary action, which began in the building where they worked at 190 North State Street in downtown Chicago. As Newton related to Ted Okuda and Mark Yurkiw in their book *Chicago TV Horror Shows: From Shock Theatre to Svengoolies*:

Bruce Newton as Frankenstein's Monster and Ronny Born as a mummy stalk
through the woods on their way to publicize WBKB-TV's new Saturday night
program *Shock Theatre.*

Me, Ronny, and Art Hern — who was one of the pirates on *The Happy Pirates* —
would put on monster masks and try to scare the folks who worked at the station. They knew it was us, so they went along with the gag. Then we'd go over
to the Tribune Building down on Michigan Avenue; we'd walk around and scare
the women in the newspaper office until we were thrown out. That's what happens when three big kids get their hands on monster masks [*laughs*].

At the same time this gruesome threesome was scaring people at WBKB, they
passed out fliers promoting the new television series.

Their promoting did not end in downtown Chicago.

On another day, the Frankenstein Monster, again played by Newton,
accompanied by Hern as the Wolf Man (although his mask looked more like
the face of a caveman), Ronny Born as a mummy and also a newcomer dubbed
"The White Widow Spider" (possibly played by model Dorothy Johnson,
who was already part of the *Shock Theatre* cast; see cover montage for photograph), the city's targeted Lincoln Park Zoo where they visited some caged
wolves, among other non-human residents.

That same day the monstrous quartet invaded Grant Park and the Egyptian section of the Chicago Natural History Museum (now the Field Museum) where they met a real (but dead) 2,8000-year-old mummy Egyptian named Harwa. According to Richard A. Martin in his 1940 museum published booklet *Mummies*, Harwa was "the keeper of the stores on a large agricultural estate of the Twenty-second Dynasty ... resting in his inner coffin." For a number of previous years, in the 1940s and 1950s, Harwa had his own dark place in the Egyptian hall where people could see him X-rayed. Today, though, he only served as a prop to help promote that night's *Shock Theatre* debut.

The two events were nicely covered in "It's a Perfectly Miserable Day," a photo spread published in the Saturday magazine supplement of the *Chicago American* newspaper the morning of *Shock Theatre*'s debut.

The Windy City had been warned. By now the city's population, or at least that part of it that loved old horror movies, would be watching.

5

Shock Waves Shake Chicago

On January 11, 1958, Marvin introduced to his television audience the original *Dracula* starring Bela Lugosi, the classic that started off the first wave of sound-era horror movies. Based on the famous novel by Bram Stoker, the movie followed the vampire Count Dracula, who comes to England seeking new victims and setting his hypnotic eyes on a young woman, before being tracked down and destroyed by a wooden stake driven through his heart.

Marvin, trying to talk, is also attempting to stop Dear from screaming. When everything fails, he yells at her, "Shut up, will you!"

Finally, she stops making noise.

"You just can't treat them nicely. Hello, I'm Marvin. Excuse me for a moment. Ready, gentlemen?"

An off-screen orchestra begins tuning up.

Marvin wants to sing, but the musicians drown him out. Taking out a revolver, Marvin fires and the music slows to a crawl.

"Ever get one of those days when nothing seems to go right? Anyway, I'm going to sing." As he begins to warm up his voice, Dear screams again. Marvin says, "I'm sorry, Dear. Rudy Vallee will never make a comeback."

Then, to the familiar tune of Al Jolson and Saul Chaplin's classic "Anniversary Song," Marvin sings [the lyrics were furnished by program director Dan Schuffman]:

"Oh, how I sighed on the night you were dead....

I vowed my true love, so I bashed in your head.

The Funeral March was so very sweet....

But your casket was short, so I cut off your feet.

(chorus)

Now I look back and see what I've done....

I think it'd be better if I'd used a gun...."

After a commercial, Marvin informs his audience, "Tonight's story is *Dracula*, the story of a man who drinks to forget. Actually, what he drank never helped him remember what he drank to forget. Dracula is a guy who loves to drink Bloody Suzannes. They're like Bloody Marys, except that there's more blood. *Dracula* is the story of a man with tired blood ... and what he drinks wakes him up. He's going to give blood too — to the Red Cross — they need it. Now, how shall we start our story? I think Westerns have quite an effect on TV, so let's use a stagecoach."

The movie *Dracula* opened with a horse-drawn coach on a road in the mountains of Transylvania, and Chicago viewers were again treated to another night of *Shock Theatre.*

Behind the Screams

By the time *Dracula* played on *Shock Theatre,* the show's opening — with its lightning, old house, music, screams and sound effects — had become familiar to regular watchers.

The lightning that opened the program had been seen before (and would be seen again) in some of the movies shown on *Shock Theatre.* It was what is called a "stock shot," purchased from

FIRST TV SHOWING
TONIGHT 10 PM

DRACULA BELA LUGOSI DAVID MANNERS

COUNT DRACULA, THE HUMAN VAMPIRE ... HE WAS THE GRAND MASTER OF THE UNDEAD CREATURES OF DARKNESS!

SHOCK THEATRE CHANNEL 7 WBKB

Another full-page *TV Guide* ad, this one is publicizing the classic Universal horror movie *Dracula.*

a stock footage library. This particular bit of stock footage had already appeared in countless movies before the folks at WBKB made use of it. Many viewers seeing that shot — the lightning suggesting, in a way, the lengthy fingers of some ghostly skeletal hand — assumed it to be authentic.

But according to Kenneth Strickfaden, the electrical wizard who invented the elaborate sparking and whirling gadgets that brought the laboratories in the Frankenstein series and so many other movies to electrical life, it was a special effect that he had created. As Strickfaden told the author around the mid–1970s, he had devised the effect for the 1935 Universal movie *Bride of Frankenstein.* He did not, however, reveal any details as to how he had achieved the effect.

Like the lightning film clip, the music also originated in old movies. Acquired from a music library, it comprised two cues married together to become *Shock Theatre's* opening theme. The first music cue, consisting of a blaring series of descending tones, was titled "Weird Incident" (catalogued as Queens Hall C-162); the second, a more mellow and lower-register cue, was named "Sword of Damocles" (Mood Music 016). The screams, like the music, had been often heard before, and were readily available on sound-effects recordings.

The haunted house was not some real building but a miniature.

The words "Shock Theatre" that suddenly appeared superimposed over the shot of the house were lined up in front of the miniature over a sheet of glass, which someone shattered off camera.

The first view of the *Shock Theatre* cellar that viewers got was the window, the camera pulling back to reveal the set. The set, made to look like a combination dungeon and mad scientist's laboratory, was rather spartanly furnished, with a table, hanging chains, spiderwebs and other appropriate items, many of them acquired from the almost always reliable Treasure Chest. As the series progressed, other items would be added to the set's décor, including an electric chair and a skeleton. Joy Bennett told Okuda and Yurkiw, "Most of the props we had to buy ourselves, with the exception of the background set — cellar, dungeon, stairs, etc. — which Frank Oakley, who was also a WBKB staff member, was able to build."

While the *Shock Theatre* set was being built and props considered, the skits featuring Marvin and his

Terry Bennett *sans* Marvin glasses with the miniature haunted house that opened each *Shock Theatre* program. The name of the show would appear on a pane of glass placed in front of the house, then shatter.

The *Shock Theatre* dungeon set designed by Frank Oakley. The area towards the left shows the set after it was expanded for the *Shocktail Party* segment, complete with its all-purpose "mad science" machine (courtesy Bruce Newton).

female foil had to be concocted. *Shock Theatre* being mostly Terry's creation, he with occasional comments and suggestions from Joy — wrote the scripts for *Shock Theatre*. Kerry Bennett noted,

—ɯ—

"My mom may have had an idea or two, but the scripts were written mainly by my dad. My mom told me that she remembered my dad writing the scripts at home on the typewriter." Joy told Rick Thomas, "Our show was different in that humor was very much a part of every skit, and then we had to act around the mistakes that one can make on a show that is done live without a script of any kind."

Actually, in *Shock Theatre*'s early days at least, Terry did write scripts of a sort for *Shock Theatre* beginning with its December 7 premiere. These were not, however, the detailed, traditionally structured, perfectly typed scripts typical of those written for most television shows.

No two *Shock Theatre* scripts looked quite the same. Some scripts were typed, others were handwritten, and all of them were heavily marked up with Terry's myriad corrections, additions and deletions, some of them presumably

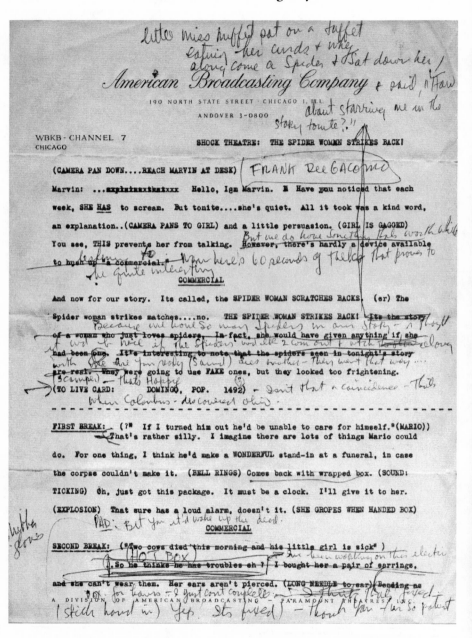

A page of the original script typed by Terry Bennett for the *Shock Theatre* presentation of *The Spider Woman Strikes Back* (courtesy Kerry Bennett).

scribbled just moments before air time, to make the skits tighter and better. A *Shock Theatre* script might turn up at the studio on standard typewriter paper, on official American Broadcasting Company office stationery, even, in at least one instance, on note paper for the Broadcaster' Promotion Association Inc.'s "BPA Second Annual Seminar" held at Chicago's Sheraton Hotel.

Often arrows scrawled by Terry indicated moves that the actors and/or the cameras should make. Some scripts, like the one Terry hand-scribed on the BPA paper for the program's showing of *Son of Frankenstein*, included a cartoon he had sketched of the Frankenstein Monster.

Shock Theatre had three directors, Dick Locke, Richie Victor and George Paul, and was, as Newton recalled to Thomas, shot with "a couple of cameras."

Regarding wardrobe, Marvin's "formal wear" (as his black outfit was described in the show's end credits) was provided by Gingiss Brothers, a Chicago clothier since 1936 (now defunct). The origin of Marvin's thick-lensed glasses, however, remains a mystery. As reported by Terry and Joy's son Kerry Bennett, the spectacles bear no markings indicating where they were manufactured or obtained.

Rehearsals for *Shock Theatre* were about as structured as Terry's "scripts." Joy, who early in 1958 would join the cast of the show, described for Ted Okuda and Mark Yurkiw what typically passed for a "rehearsal":

> We weren't afforded the luxury of rehearsal time; for the benefit of the director and the technical crew, we'd do a walk-through about 15 minutes before we went on the air. We would have a premise but we ad-libbed our way through every-thing. This was live television, and you had to be prepared for any contingen-cies, like malfunctioning props. Terry was such a pro that he could ad-lib his way through any situation.

To Rick Thomas, Joy said, "We would have a walk-through for about 15 min-utes before we went on camera. It was mostly for the positioning of the camera and the boom, lights and props had to be set."

The program's crew, Newton told Thomas, included a producer whose main job seemed to be keeping track of the commercials; a "shader," who controlled the lighting; and a "switcher," who made the switch from one cam-era to the other. The activities of all these people — including stage hands, musicians and sound effects people, comprising the show's very minimal crew — were overseen by the director.

In Print

As *Shock Theatre* continued airing into the early months of 1958, its pop-ularity always growing, the program began to garner more notice. Terry soon enjoyed seeing his name and photographs printed in a variety of periodicals.

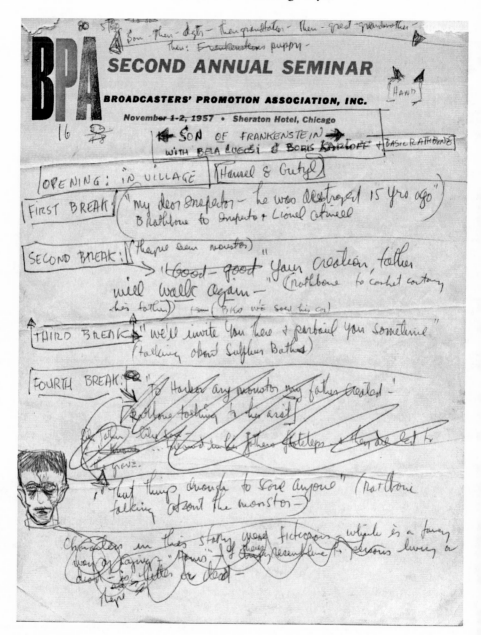

Original script handwritten (and cartoon-drawn) by Terry Bennett for the night *Shock Theatre* ran *Son of Frankenstein* (courtesy Kerry Bennett).

The February 6, 1958 edition of *Pictorial Living*, the Sunday supplement of the *Chicago American* newspaper, ran an impressive feature story written by Ernest Tucker titled "A Real Cool Ghoul!" with photographs by Arnold Tolchin. Among the photos was a nice picture of Terry dressed as Marvin, *sans* glasses, standing beside his lovely wife Joy, who often visited the set.

Tucker's article described Bennett's character:

> Marvin does his job well. A gnomish little fellow, peering through a pair of impossibly thick specs, he is reminiscent of Peter Lorre in one of his less humanitarian moods. In a voice best described as a sepulchral tenor, Marvin talks a little about the week's social events: the danses macabre, walpurgisnachts and fiendish orgies which make up his social calendar.

It wasn't long before publicity for *Shock Theatre* went national. Giving Chicago's *Shock Theatre* notoriety across the 48 states, *TV Guide*, the country's leading publication posting television schedules and articles about TV shows and stars, included a feature in its March 29, 1958, issue titled "What a Revoltin' Development!" Describing the impact of "'Horror Show' emcees in becoming a national phenomenon," the article not only discussed Marvin, as well as other TV horror hosts, but opened with a photo of a leering Terry as his creation.

Just two months after the *TV Guide* piece appeared, *Life* (issue cover dated May 26), then the nation's most widely read magazine, offered "Night Harbingers of Horror," a similar pictorial article. Marvin wasn't featured in the spread (although a number of photographs had been taken by a *Life* photographer); in the letters column of the next issue, reader Sue Ellen Park of Evanston, Illinois, inquired, "What happened to that ghoulish

Terry Bennett as Marvin on one of the early episodes of *Shock Theatre* (courtesy Kerry Bennett).

announcer from Chicago named 'Marvin'?" An editor replied, "'Marvin' is Terry Bennett of WBKB-TV in Chicago. His favorite subject of torture is his wife Joy, shown in the picture above." The accompanying photograph depicted a grinning Marvin in the act of hanging Dear (by now played by Joy Bennett) by her pretty neck.

The August 16, 1958, issue of another national periodical, the much respected *Saturday Evening Post*, featured the article "TV's Midnight Madness," wherein author Roul Tunley wrote, "In Chicago, a million viewers a week faithfully watch a chilling comic called Marvin introduce movies with such remarks as: 'This is the story of Frankenstein, a story that poses the question: Can a monster over thirty-five find happiness with a playmate?'" The article included a photograph of Marvin holding up a sign promoting the show over Dear's face.

With coverage in periodicals of the stature of *TV Guide*, *Life* and *The Saturday Evening Post*, publicity for *Shock Theatre* just couldn't be any better.

Other kinds of magazines — ones geared toward young fans of horror movies and monsters — also took note of *Shock Theatre* and its master of scaremonies. Forrest J Ackerman's *Famous Monsters of Filmland* #2 (1958) featured the article "TerrorVision," by "punmeister" Ackerman *sans* byline. Like the piece in *TV Guide*, it opened with a photograph of "chicago's [*sic*] shocker," noting, "Marvin the Near-Sighted Madman is the monicker of Terry Bennett, Chicago host of *SHOCK* on WBKB." According to this article, Bennett had "taken to his role like a ghoul out of a grave!" and, on a weekly basis, terrified an attractive blonde "who scarcely enjoys having her tootsies toasted, her fingers roasted, her brain fried, and her tonsils squeezed for grape juice, but watcha gonna do when 'that's the way the monster mumbles.'"

Dead Letters

Although only a small number of *Shock Theatre* shows had aired by early 1958, the show's fan base was growing exponentially — and the curiosity of those devoted followers of the show, like their numbers, was also increasing.

Letters began filling the mailboxes of WBKB. Missives inquiring about the show and characters also began to flood the various "letters to the editor" departments of Chicago's local newspapers. Some of these letters were published and even answered.

> Please tell me these facts about Terry Bennett. When is his birthday? What sport does he like and does he have a favorite food? Is he left-handed or right-handed?
>
> — Ruth Ann Putz,
> LaGrange, Ill.

Dorothy Johnson doing one of her modeling gigs. Johnson was the first person to play Dear (aka "Her").

Terry's birthday is April 25th. He says he likes baseball, boxing and eating shrimps. As a ventriloquist, Terry is left-handed "most of the time. But I throw lefty, and write righty," he said.

"Dear" Number One

There were also questions about the young woman, face never seen, who was murdered, maimed or mutilated each Saturday night, only to return the following week — even on the same episode of the program — restored back to her lovely and healthy self. One such letter was answered with the following facts:

> Terry Bennett has an assistant, a red-haired model named Dorothy Johnson, whose sole function is to scream. Terry rips off women's fingernails (false) and lights his cigarets with them. On one occasion, he cut out a woman's heart (slab of beef liver), listened to it beat and sent it to a Lonely Hearts Club. He also serves "shocktails" made of embalming fluid.

Johnson, the original Dear was attractive, had experience as a professional model and, even better for WBKB and *Shock Theatre*'s tight budget, she was already a Channel 7 employee . That meant that she, like Bruce Newton, Ronny Born, Art Hern and even Terry Bennett, could be shifted around to perform a number of disparate duties, like playing opposite Marvin.

In order to keep the budget even more manageable, the WBKB powers-that-be decided that, rather than paying the union AFTRA (American Federation of Television and Recording Artists) minimum wages which that union required for a speaking role on a television show, the character of Dear would have no lines. Indeed, the only sounds the character would ever make would be moans, shrieks, gasps or, more often, screams.

Up through the earliest 1958 *Shock Theatre* broadcasts, Marvin subjected Dear, as played by Johnson, to a Grand Guignol array of his gleeful horrors. For example, in one break from the night's movie he attacked her head, seen only from behind as usual, with a meat cleaver. Later, always trying to be helpful, Marvin corrected the damage he'd caused Dear's skull by sewing it back together with a needle and thread.

> Marvin sneaks down the dungeon stairs, ready to speak. On this night, however, the expected opening scream is not heard — not at first, anyway.
> Finally, Dear makes her appearance, screaming her head off, then falling, apparently dead.
> "She's such a ham. Hello, I'm Marvin," says the man with the thick spectacles. Proudly, he begins to show off his attire. "She got me this suit. She got it from a store that's located out of the high-rent shopping district. It's almost ten miles north of Labrador. It's one of those places where you see across acres and acres of

Above: Marvin (Terry Bennett) takes a meat cleaver to Dear's (Dorothy Johnson) lovely head....
Below: ... then tries his best to mend the damage.

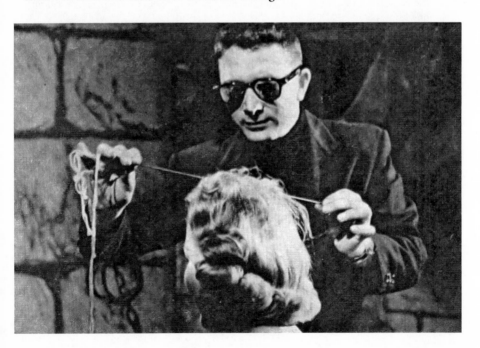

plain pipe racks. No suits, but the best-looking pipe racks in town. But she tries to make me happy. You might say she's the flower of womanhood. No wonder she's wilted. When we first met, she gave me a dog for a gift. I liked him so much I let him sleep with me. I know it's unsanitary, but the dog got used to it. Anyway, she's just like a woman ... always talking and talking. It's so annoying. Not at all like our commercials."

Following the first commercial, Marvin explains, "Tonight's story is the *Were-Wolf of London*. As you'll see in our story, the werewolf makes many, many trips. No wonder the London bridges are falling down.

"Because our story takes place in London, our characters speak with an English accent ... but thank goodness it's not too heavy an accent. If it were any heavier we'd need subtitles. Our story is very different. It's strangely different. It's about a man who becomes a wolf."

Marvin pauses for a few moments ... in thought.

"Come to think of it, it's not very different at all. Many people think that the werewolf comes about because his mother was frightened by a wolf. This is not true. These things just don't happen. Although I know one mother who was scared by a bear ... and the baby was born with bare feet." He laughs, hysterically.

"Of course you know London is very foggy. I was once in a place that was foggier than London. Unfortunately it was so foggy I never did find out where it was."

Marvin moves over to a globe of the world. "Oh, for those of you who wonder what shape the world is in ... it's in pretty bad shape." He spins the globe, the camera moving in closer. "Round and round she goes ... where she stops, no one knows."

Thus *WereWolf of London*, the sixth movie to be shown on *Shock Theatre*, began on January 18 of the new year.

As the movie progressed to its first break, ending with actor Warner Oland in Japanese makeup as Dr. Yogami warning star Henry Hull, as the movie's title character, that men suffering the werewolf curse are doomed, Marvin was again on screen.

"No men are actually doomed," says Marvin, "unless, of course, they get married. I wouldn't say that normally, but I suppose a lot of you will write in with such a load of letters that it'll almost kill the mailman. And that's why I mention it.

Actually, marriage is an institution. And according to some of you, you have to be crazy to get into it. Which reminds me. Most people think wives always start arguments. But don't you believe it! Although I know one couple getting married. The groom said, 'I do.' And the wife said, 'Oh, no you don't!'

"Authorities say marriage compromise is best, but we know compromise is like pulling teeth. Which reminds me...

Marvin yanks from Dear's mouth a pair of chattering teeth [plastic wind-up teeth bought, as usual, at the Treasure Chest] and sets them down on the table. "See what I mean? Yatatat ... yatatat.... That's all they do!"

"Who's That Guy Standing Next to Rondo Hatton?"

For some inexplicable reason, other than the comedy potential of the virtually unknown name, Marvin — or Terry Bennett, anyway — developed an ongoing fascination with a screen presence named Rondo Hatton

On January 5, 1958, *Shock Theatre* showed *The Spider Woman Strikes Back*, a 1946 Universal production in which Hatton played Mario, the mute servant of the Spider Woman (portrayed by Gale Sondergaard).

Hatton was an "actor," using the term in its most generous sense, of very limited abilities. He had appeared in a number of movies made during the 1930s and 1940s, most of

The last full-page *TV Guide* advertisement to promote a specific *Shock Theatre* movie.

them of the "B" category. He was cast by Universal Pictures in the Creeper role not for any real thespian abilities, but solely for his strange look. Hatton suffered from acromegaly, a disease that altered his features drastically, lengthening his face and enlarging his hands.

Universal took advantage of Hatton's physical features and Hatton accepted the easy employment. He didn't really have to act to play the Creeper, just lumber about and, on occasion, strangle someone or break their spine. For Universal, using Hatton in a horror movie meant saving time and, even better, money. They finally had someone who could play a "monster" without first having to spend several tedious hours being changed into one by the studio's cantankerous make-up maestro Jack Pierce.

Marvin's first mention of Rondo Hatton was on January 18, 1958, the night that *Shock Theatre* first showed *WereWolf of London*. Following that movie's fade-out, Marvin told his audience that next week's offering was to be *The Spider Woman Strikes Back*, starring Gale Sondergaard and Kirby Grant.

> Marvin pauses after announcing the movies' two major stars, then continues, "And the big surprise of the evening, one of the most outstanding stars you've ever seen.... Lots of fan clubs all over the country for him ... [*pause*] Ah.... Everyone knows him. He's one of the biggest stars there are [*pause*]. He's, ah [*pause*] He's written up in every movie magazine and fan club magazine there is, he's...."
> Marvin pauses again, as if trying to remember the name, finally saying it slowly.
> "Rondo Hatton. And you'll see him along with everyone else in *The Spider Woman Strikes Back*."

After that original announcement, Marvin mentioned Rondo Hatton so many times that the name became ubiquitous, indeed a running joke on *Shock Theatre*. And whenever Hatton turned up in one of the motion pictures shown on the program, Marvin was certain to make a big deal of it.

When Marvin showed *The Spider Woman Strikes Back*, after the scene wherein the Spider Woman stated that if she turned Mario out, her servant would be unable to care for himself, Marvin commented, "That's rather silly. I imagine there are lots of things Mario could do. For one thing, I think he'd make a wonderful stand-in at a funeral, in case the corpse couldn't make it."

On June 14, following the fade-out of that night's movie *The Cat Creeps*, Marvin announced that next week's offering would be *House of Horrors*. Best of all, the film was actually going to *star* none other than Rondo Hatton. Upon realizing that again his audience hadn't a clue as to who Hatton was, Marvin related a phony anecdote of the time that, in Russia, Nikita Khrushchev was about to give a speech before an enormous crowd. Beside the Russian prime minister stood the one and only Rondo Hatton. According to Marvin's account, before Khrushchev could utter a single word of his speech, someone in the crowd raised his fist and hollered, "Hey, who's that guy standing next to Rondo Hatton?"

House of Horrors was made the same year as *The Spider Woman Strikes Back*; and like the latter film, it was a minor entry in Universal Pictures horror canon. The Creeper, as played by Hatton (heavily padded to make the rather smallish man look huge) was a brutish, stalking killer of very few words. One reason that the Creeper was so laconic is simple. Hatton was arguably the worst actor working at the studio.

The Creeper would make one additional screen appearance in *The Brute*

Man, made by Universal but released by PRC in 1946. That movie was not, however, included among the Screen Gems titles.

Marvin introduced *House of Horrors* like this:

> "Our story tonight is a true one. Nothing has been changed except the facts. It's the story of what happens to a peaceful, happy family of two when the mothers-in-law move in with them. It's called *House of Horrors* and is not to be confused with the book of the same name, which is almost as bad as our story.
>
> "The hero of tonight's story is a familiar name to all movie-goers and show business enthusiasts — Rondo Hatton!" Marvin is amazed. "You've never heard of him? Why, he's just as famous as Irving Maxwell, and who hasn't heard of him?"

House of Horrors began, continuing along to its first break, ending with a scene in which the Creeper snaps the backbone of a female victim. When Marvin returned, he was reacting to the murder.

> "I've always wondered why anyone would want to snap a woman's spine. Probably because she hadn't heard of Rondo Hatton."
>
> Marvin goes over to Dear, still trying to convince her that everyone has heard of Rondo Hatton, but his attempt soon proves futile. "All right, let's stop arguing," he tells her. "This has gone far enough. I'm willing to forget this argument. You want to bury the hatchet?" Dear thinks over his question and nods. Smiling, Marvin turns around. The woman — for once *not* the victim — raises a hatchet and buries it in his back.
>
> "That's not what I meant by burying the hatchet," he says, reacting to the tool. "Dear, where'd you get that? Say, that 'Goldfine' fellow [i.e., Bernard Goldfine, then involved in a scandal in which he offered gifts in return for favors to presidential advisor Sherman Adams] gives gifts to everybody, doesn't he?"

By the time *House of Horrors* ended, Marvin had been shrunk to tiny size, the result of accepting from Dear a shocktail having the power to reduce a human being. Dear was holding Marvin, concealed from view, beneath the fingers of her clenched hand:

> "Now, Dear...." Complains Marvin [*in voice-over*], "you've got me in the palm of your hand. The joke's over."
>
> Dear sticks a finger of her free hand into her fist.
>
> "Ouch! Don't you ever cut your nails? You gave me a part in my hair that goes right down to my neck. Now, Dear, you've just got to let me out. I've got to get back to normal size."
>
> Again she pokes a finger into her fist.
>
> "Ouch! Say, Dear, would you mind opening your fist a little? It's getting very hard to breathe in here."
>
> She laughs and clenches her fist tighter.
>
> "Dear, you're clenching it tighter. That's not what I mean."
>
> Finally, laughing, she opens her fist, but only slightly — and sawdust falls from it.

Joy Bennett, Terry's wife, visits the *Shock Theatre* set. Soon she would assume the role of Dear and her face — like Dorothy Johnson's — would be hidden from view.

"Now look what you've done." Marvin complains. "I'm falling all to pieces. Whatever would Rondo Hatton say?"

The Shocks Continue

When on February 1 Marvin ran *The Invisible Man*, a Universal film of 1933 based on the novel by H. G. Wells, he commented on a scene in which the title character, played by Claude Rains, tosses a man down a flight of stairs.

"Hmmm ... he throws him down those stairs as if he's his stepbrother [*laughs*].

"Well, by now you know how the Invisible Man looks. Actually, no one can turn invisible, so please put down your chemistry sets."

Marvin holds up a syringe and lets Dear, who is sitting nearby, get a look at it.

"Oh, this, by the way is a hypodermic needle. And I'm not John Cameron Swayze. I filled it with my own little concoction." He rams the needle into the woman. "See...? And it stops blood clogging, too."

Dear's fate was soon to change dramatically. She was about to undergo a major transformation, including a new hair color and a somewhat different relationship with Marvin.

However, before that new "faceless face" appeared on the show, it would be seen each weekday morning — unmasked, although heavily made-up — on a very different kind of show targeted at a considerably younger audience.

6

Present and Future Shocks

Marvin liked to refer to the horror movies he showed as "comedies," "musicals" and even "cartoons."

On February 8, 1958, *Shock Theatre* premiered *The Black Cat*, a 1934 Universal movie inspired by the Edgar Allan Poe classic, starring Boris Karloff and Bela Lugosi. It was significant in that it was celebrated as the first appearance of the *Frankenstein* and *Dracula* superstars Karloff and Lugosi, respectively, on the same screen. Less faithful to Poe than *Murders in the Rue Morgue*, already seen on *Shock Theatre*, *The Black Cat* was an original tale including satanic worship, cults, sadism and even hints of incest and necrophilia.

In short, an ideal "cartoon" for *Shock Theatre's* ninth telecast, right up Marvin's proverbial alley.

Marvin sits at his desk. Dear is also at the desk, slumped over as if dead. Marvin shakes her, trying to awaken the woman. She stirs, wakes up, screams, then goes back into her slump.

"She asked me to awaken her when our story started. Hello, 'Shock Absorbers,' I'm Marvin. I'd like to read our nursery rhyme for tonight."

The poem, a parody of a well-known children's verse, has been sent in by *Shock Theatre* fan Bill Feret:

"Humpey Lumpey sat in a crypt.

"And all of a sudden, he suddenly slipped.

"And falling from that terrible height,

"Everyone had scrambled eggs that night."

Marvin now introduces the night's movie. "Our story tonight was suggested by the Veterinarian Society. It's called *The Black Cat*, and is not to be confused with a commercial which is due right now...."

The commercial over, Marvin continues, "Our heroes in tonight's story are Bela Lugosi and Boris Karloff. They almost weren't in tonight's story. Each wanted the other's part. They finally came to an agreement, though. They tossed a body in the air. It came down 'heads' and Karloff got the part.

"Just look at Karloff. You'd never believe that he's an excellent musician, would you? No foolin' ... here's a picture of him at one of his concertos...."

The Black Cat commenced with a scene at a railroad depot, accompanied by the rousing opening strains of Franz Liszt's Hungarian Rhapsody No. 3.

Many Voices, Many Characters

Terry Bennett was blessed with many talents.

He could write, act, sing, perform magic, play the piano, do comedy, do celebrity impressions and draw, and his creative abilities probably didn't stop there. But, first and foremost, Terry was a ventriloquist, and a fine one at that. Alas, *Shock Theatre* was not the kind of venue that gave him much opportunity to display his ventriloquial abilities.

In the early weeks of 1958, Terry and Joy, began appearing on another show that he created, *The Jobblewocky Place*. This hour-long children's program aired live on Channel 7 every Monday through Friday starting also at 10 o'clock — although in the morning.

It was on this new show that some of Terry's many talents — including ventriloquism, comedy, writing, producing, acting and singing — truly shone.

These smaller *TV Guide* advertisements became the norm for *Shock Theatre*.

Terry Bennett flanked by his wooden "friends" Timothy Timber (left) and Red Flannels (right), both made by Frank Marshall (courtesy Kerry Bennett).

Terry played himself, again wearing a turtleneck sweater — not the black one he wore as Marvin, but a beige garment emblazoned on the front with a huge J. The show was aimed at young children but, as things later turned out, would also be watched by older kids and adults who appreciated Terry's witty and often quite sophisticated humor. He even composed the show's theme song and lyrics:

> Igglehocky, trobblebocky, that's a lot of Jobblewocky,
> And it means why don't we take a little walk.
> Igglehocky, trobblebocky, that's a lot of Jobblewocky,
> Everyone who's anyone knows Jobblewocky talk.
> If you want to learn how to do it
> Practice in front of a mirror
> Every morning, every noon, and almost every night.
> Igglehocky, trobblebocky, that's a mountain called the Rocky,
> Just like eating crackers with a spoon and fork.

Joy, heavily made-up to resemble a life-sized doll, played a recurring role on *The Jobblewocky Place*— that of Terry's ward, a precocious 12-year-old named Pamela Puppet. Co-starring with the Bennetts on the new show were his long-time wooden partners Red Flannels and Timothy Timber.

Joy Bennett in her other TV persona as Pamela Puppet, here with Terry Bennett and dummy Red Flannels on the ABC-TV morning children's show *The Jobblewocky Place* (photograph Kerry Bennett).

The Jobblewocky Place also introduced a new cast of zany characters. One, Rusty Hinges, was another figure created by Terry's friend Frank Marshall. However, most of *The Jobblewocky Place*'s denizens were the handiwork of the always reliable Bruce Newton. Among these Newton-made inhabitants of this new magical realm, all speaking by way of Terry's ventriloquial skills, were Mr. Head (a disembodied head in a box inspired by Pedro, famed ventriloquist Señor Wenses' talking head character), who constantly told Bennett to "Close the door," Uncle Louie (a talking picture), Bertram Turtle and Mr. Engineer.

Most impressive of all, in terms of Terry demonstrating both his ventriloquial talents and also his impeccable sense of comic timing, was his performances with a trio of heads set atop a shelf—one apparently human, the others the aptly named Dicky Duck and Danny Dog. They were known collectively (yet rather inaccurately) as the Three Smart Men. Terry's comedy bits with the Three Smart Men constituted an amazing *tour de force*, with Terry switching from himself to any of the three with such speed, and without missing a single beat, that it almost seemed as if more than one head, his own included, were talking at the same time.

The Jobblewocky Place was perfectly described by Okuda and Yurkiw in their book as "an innovative children's program that combined the educational agenda of *Ding Dong School* with the good-natured zaniness of Soupy Sales and the skewered imagination of Ernie Kovacs."

The show was another Terry Bennett–created immediate hit, praised by critics and eventually garnering three Emmy award nominations. Joy told Okuda and Yurkiw that *Jobblewocky Place* "gave us great satisfaction because we had a loyal preschool audience that we felt our show catered to in a loving and educational way. We probably had a more positive feeling toward *Jobblewocky Place* because it brought us personal rewards."

The New Dear

Joy continued to visit the *Shock Theatre* set where she watched her husband work. Her presence behind the show's cameras eventually accomplished more than just observing. Terry's young wife had already tallied her own healthy résumé of stage and nightclub appearances working alongside her husband .

As she explained in Okuda and Yurkiw's book:

For a few shows in the beginning, the station used a staff member named Dorothy Johnson. That way, it did not cost them anything extra. However, because of our ability to work so well together, Terry talked them into using me for *Shock Theatre*. This caused the station a bit of concern. I was playing the part

Dear, now played by Joy Bennett, helps Marvin (husband Terry Bennett) to promote *Shock Theatre.*

of a 12-year-old girl, Pamela Puppet, on our morning children's show, *Jobble-wocky Place*, and they felt it was not good for the audience to know that I was also part of *Shock Theatre*.

At first Joy's addition to *Shock Theatre* cost WBKB a little more money because, unlike Johnson, she was a freelancer rather than a staff employee. Nevertheless, this increase to the program's budget inevitably paid off. Dear was gradually enriched by Joy's performances and revamping of the character, and would become as popular as Marvin himself. With an actual entertainer and not just a pretty model in the role, Dear evolved, each week winning more on-camera time. While the original Dear spent most of her air time either sitting or lying down, doing nothing while Marvin worked his fiendish machinations upon her, Joy's Dear became more of a participant in the skits.

Also, Dear was soon heard mouthing a kind of very rudimentary "baby talk," producing sounds that made much of what she was trying to communicate somewhat comprehensible. And while Dorothy Johnson's original Dear was usually fairly quiet, except for her occasional moans, groans and screams, Joy's Dear, after a while, could get downright noisy! All the while, of course, Joy was careful to make her voice distinct from that of Pamela Puppet.

With Joy playing Dear, audiences also got to see more of her, although that "more" did not include showing her face. Now the cameras would show Dear from the side and even the front instead of just from behind. To keep her face hidden, she began to wear a lacey mask that added visually to her screen presence.

Joy's joining the *Shock Theatre* cast was not without its drawbacks. Eventually the station revoked her freelance status and hired her as another staff employee. Therefore, like her husband and other *Shock Theatre* cast members, Joy had to do just about anything the WBKB brass dictated her to do.

Nevertheless, Terry and his new co-star were not restricted much by Sterling Quinlan, at least as far as their creativity was concerned. "We had a lot of latitude in those days," Joy told Rick Thomas in *Filmfax*, "and could pretty well call our own shots."

On February 21, *Shock Theatre* showed the 1940 movie *The Mummy's Hand*, the first of Universal Pictures series of "B" pictures featuring Kharis (played in only this entry by cowboy star Tom Tyler), a different bandaged horror from the one Boris Karloff had played eight years earlier.

> "Hello, I'm Marvin. This is my new ghoul fiend. I dug her up. I'd like to thank you for your nice letters."
> Marvin picks up a sheet of paper and begins to read (the parody possibly again written by fan Bill Feret)....
> "Mary had a little ghoul,

The second Dear (Joy Bennett) is the willing victim of Marvin (Terry Bennett)
on *Shock Theatre*.

"Its skin was smooth as Yu's.
"And to everything that Mary did,
"The ghoul was sure to drool!
"Which was against the law.
"And you could hear her screaming....
"With her neck inside his jaw[*laughs*]!"
Composing himself, Marvin continues, "Where shall we start our story? In
    Joliet? In a grave? Would that please you? We'd better start with a commer-
    cial...so that would please our sponsor!"
After the sponsor has his say....
"Well, now for our story. It's called ... it's called...."
A coffin opens and a hand, wrapped in bandages, emerges and gives Marvin a
    note.
"Oh, *The Mummy's Hand.*" Looking into the coffin, he observes, "Imagine
    that, a new outfit ... turtleneck bandages. Well, needless to say, our story
    takes place thousands of years ago, as you can tell by the quality of the
    film. And now let's start our 90-minute commercial for Band-Aid, *The
    Mummy's Hand....*"

During the course of *The Mummy's Hand*, the new and soon-to-be-improved
Dear was immediately at home in Marvin's dreary dungeon, where everything

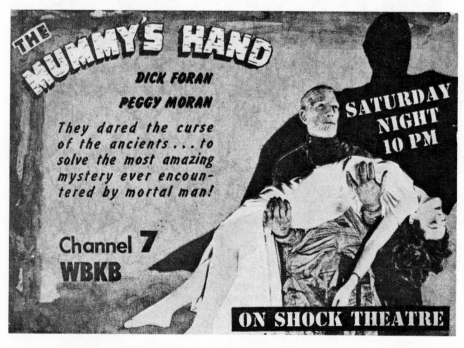

TV Guide ad for the first entry in Universal Pictures' series featuring the
mummy Kharis.

seemed to be (to use a Chicago expression usually referring to local politics) "business as usual." During the movie's first break, following a scene where an archaeologist (played by Western movie actor Dick Foran) purchases a broken vase upon which is an inscription, written in hieroglyphics, Marvin appears holding a vase....

"Oh, this is like the vase our hero just bought. This one is not broken. It's for Her for Valentine's Day. It's a surprise. She expects a new car. Here, Dear, catch...!"

He throws the vase, after which comes the sound of the vase breaking.

"Well, that proves one thing. If you care enough to give the very best — give money! Sticks and stones can break my bones, but...."

At the second break, as Foran's character, following his involvement in a barroom fight, escapes through a window....

"Why doesn't he take an ad in the 'help wanted' section? Wasn't that fight exciting? Makes you want to yell. 'What'll you have?' Seriously, I don't think they'll ever find the mummy at all ... if there is one. Actually, it's just a new sponsor who devised a novel way to help soap up tiny razor nicks."

Marvin begins to wrap the hand of Dear, who is already partially swathed in bandages. "Oh, I promised her one of those coats that look like real fur ... but couldn't get any. So I'm doing the next best thing. It's a coat that looks like real bandages."

By the next break, following a *The Mummy's Hand* scene where an Arab-type excuses himself....

Dear is stretched out on a table.

"Wait a minute," exclaims Marvin, "you can't leave now! It's commercial time! Say, you know, I'm practicing magic, too. For two weeks now I've been trying to make two rabbits disappear, but I never succeed. They always seem to outnumber me. Anyway, I just read the book *How to Saw a Woman in Half*. Tried it this morning and it worked beautifully. Here, watch...."

Marvin picks up a saw and noisily goes to work.

"Now I'll say the magic words to bring her back together ... *Shock Theatre* ... *Shock Theatre*...."

When nothing happens, he looks puzzled. "I don't understand it. I did it this morning and she went to pieces about the trick. I must be saying the wrong words. I'd better use the substitute words. They always work.... "Commercial Time ... Commercial Time...."

As another break comes in the movie, upon a scene of Kharis stalking through the woods....

Dear, out of camera range, lies in a coffin.

Marvin, still confused, looks down at his saw.

"Well, now I know where they got that joke "Who was that woman I sawed you with last night?" [*laughs*] I always knew she had a split personality. Anyway ... who would believe that the Mummy can come back to life?"

He picks up a sprinkling can and waters the coffin.

"That's ridiculous!"

A moan issues from the casket.

"Stop complaining! You need the water. How else can you swallow those plant vitamins?"

At the end of the show, following a preview trailer for next week's movie *Secret of the Blue Room*, Marvin was back again for the final wrap-up:.

"I'll tell you the secret of the Blue Room right now ... it's green!"

Dear is off-camera again, and all that indicates her presence is a length of bandages.

"Say good night, Dear. Say good night, Dear."

Noticing the bandages, he grabs the end and lights it like a fuse.

Moments later, something — or someone — unseen explodes.

Marvin looks towards camera. "Wonderful girl. She's out of this world. Goodnight."

7

Electrically Shocking Charges

On February 22,. *Shock Theatre* showed *Secret of the Blue Room*, a spooky mystery movie made by Universal Pictures in 1933, about a group of people attempting to defy a death curse by spending the night in the (supposedly) haunted "Blue Room" of a castle.

Tonight's story was suggested by the local real estate firm." "It's called The *Secret of the Blue Room*. It's a strange story ... because it's all about a room. Not a house, just a room.

A lot of you are under the impression that tonight's story is old. That's not true. Just because it was filmed with a Brownie Number Two camera has nothing at all to do with it. No film ... just the Brownie Number Two camera!

Before the movie was over, the new Dear — like her predecessor — was subjected to an array of Marvin's tortures. During the first break, after a scene in which two of the characters agree to sleep in the mysterious Blue Room....

"So they're all going to spend a night in the Blue Room," Marvin comments. "I'll have to remind the janitor to send up some heat. The furnace has been clogged up ... with ashes lately. A few friends of mine were real mad at me. They still are. They're really burned up. Well, they were always so hot-tempered anyway. But of course, if the janitor can't make it, I could always do it."

Moving over to Dear, he asks, "Did I ever show you how to tighten a lock nut?" Dear lets Marvin know that he has not. Twisting her nose with a wrench, Marvin continues, as Dear screams and shrieks:

"Well, all right, so it was your nose. But you do the exact same thing with the bolt."

By the second break, Marvin was back again at his gruesome work.

"Hello." Marvin looks around the dungeon. "This is my own little blue room. Actually, it's not a room at all. It's not even blue. It's not even mine. I keep it handy for the guests.

"Did you notice that, in our story, everybody shakes hands before going to sleep? Actually they're just counting their fingers. One of them has a unique

95

TONIGHT 10 PM

The SECRET OF THE BLUE ROOM

LIONEL ATWILL — PAUL LUKAS

Marvin, your host on SHOCK THEATRE, is also eager to learn of the secret that lurked behind the locked door.

SATURDAY NIGHT 10 P.M.

SHOCK THEATRE

CHANNEL 7   WBKB

This was the first *Shock Theatre* advertisement in *TV Guide* to use the popular image of Marvin (Terry Bennett) to publicize the show.

hobby called 'finger painting,' except he does it with someone else's fingers. You use them five times ... and then find a new friend."

Moving over to Dear, Marvin says, "Oh, are you going to take a nap?" He shakes her hand and it comes off. "My, I'm stronger than I thought I was."

In the third break, following a scene in the movie where a detective, investigating a murder, asks the other characters who was the first among them to find the dead man....

"Well, don't look at me, I didn't do it. I was in the other room chopping a chip off an old block. But I know that this detective is really smart. Why, he's solved crimes that haven't even been committed yet. But if you look at this detective real closely, you'll notice a bulge under his jacket right here."

Marvin taps the chest area of his own jacket.

"That's a gun. No, not that side, that's his ... this side."

Removing a .38 revolver from under his jacket, he continues, "This is a special gun that all police detectives use. It always helps the cops get their man. Because it fires six times and then throws rocks. Here, watch."

Marvin fires the gun once at Dear, who drops to the floor in a heap.

"You've got to stay out of the way when I'm...." he begins to tell her, then reacts with surprise. "Oh. Look, you've got an extra buttonhole in your blouse."

After *Secret of the Blue Room* ended, and following a trailer previewing next week's movie *Dracula's Daughter*, Marvin returned again, this time gripping Dear in a wrestler's stranglehold.

> "And now it's time to say good night," Marvin says, struggling for breath, I'd like to remind you that if you like ... strangleholds ... and neck stretching ... stay tuned for *Wrestling* ... following *Shock*....
> "And by the way ... tomorrow is Heart Sunday.... People will be coming around to ask for your contributions ... and I'll be around to ask for your heart.
> "Be sure to feed the wildlife ... like rabbits ... and birds.... I've been feeding the vultures....
> "And now it's time to say good night...."
> Marvin releases his grip on Dear's neck and she slumps into a chair.
> "Say good night," he tells Dear, picking up her limp arm and shaking her hand. "Good night."

Marvin Mishaps

With all of Marvin's mayhem — not to mention the props involved — mishaps were to be expected. Because *Shock Theatre* was done live, not on film or videotape, there could be no retakes when something went wrong.

Although the revolvers fired at Dear by Marvin never contained real bullets and the knives he wielded never pierced her skin, she was, on occasion, a real-life victim. In one skit that went amiss, Marvin tossed Dear into an open grave that had been fashioned on the set by Bruce Newton, and some stage hands. Marvin was then supposed to cover her by shoveling sand — in all, 50 pounds of the stuff— over her reclining body. The plan was that, for protection against the falling sand, Joy Bennett, once out of camera range, would cover herself with a sheet.

That was the plan, anyway.

Once in the grave, Joy pulled the sheet over her, according to the plan. Somehow, though, the sheet slipped away and Terry Bennett suddenly found himself dumping all of the sand onto his wife. It required the efforts of several stagehands to free her from the mess.

Another time, Dear was supposed to scream and then faint, with Joy comfortably collapsing atop a pillow. Joy managed to miss the pillow and hit the floor hard, almost knocking herself out cold in the process.

In yet another incident, Marvin came at Dear with an ax. When Terry swung the ax, the handle struck hard against Joy's leg, leaving a nasty bruise.

On March 8, *Shock Theatre* screened *The Invisible Ray*, a 1936 Universal opus starring Boris Karloff and Bela Lugosi, wherein the Karloff character, his body poisoned by an element from outer space, utilizes his touch of death to eliminate his enemies. Marvin that night used a far more physical method of dispatching Dear during one of the movie's breaks. It came following a scene in which a scientist noted to his colleagues that their expeditions have never been under the auspices of any organization.

> "And it's a good thing, too," agrees Marvin, "or they'd be investigated by some Senate Investigating Committee.
> "Say, wasn't it wonderful the way they took a trip through space? Of course, on their way back they passed a Sputnik. So, they're going on a trip to Africa ... the land of excitement, or mystery, of Mau Maus. But she once went to Africa and said that those Mau Maus aren't so bad ... or so dangerous. Isn't that right, Dear?"
> Marvin goes over to Dear ... who is missing her head!
> "Hmmmm.... That's what she gets for rubbing that vanishing cream on her face."

Dr. Bennett and Mr. Hyde?

In 1958, Terry Bennett may have seemed to be leading two lives, hosting an innocent and highly regarded children's show by day and a gruesome horror show by night; and Terry seemed to undergo this transformation without needing to take any kind of smoking and bubbling potion.

Some viewers must have been "shocked" that year to discover that *Shock Theatre* emceer Terry and Joy were also delighting kiddies in the morning five days a week on *The Jobblewocky Place*. On March 10, to explain this apparent schizophrenic situation, WBKB, with corporate tongue in cheek, sent out an official press release:

> Terry Bennett, star of WBKB's *Shock Theatre* and *Jobblewocky Place*," is a "Dr. Jekyll and Mr. Hyde."
> This is the era of psychoanalysis and the split personality, but no one in Chicago TV has manifested such outward signs of transition as WBKB's Terry Bennett.
> Terry, a mild-mannered young man with a subtle sense of humor, is host of both the waggish *Jobblewocky Place* and the macbre [*sic*] *Shock Theatre.*
> In *Jobblewocky Place*, Terry appears as a witty jester who more times than not is a foil for Red Flannels and Timothy Timber, puppets conceived in the lighter, carefree lobe of Bennett's brain.
> The children who enter into the fantastic world daily (10–11 A.M.) form a solid group of wide-eyed worshippers who think of Terry as their "big brother," who has the wizardry to take them into the enchanted "Jobblewocky Place" where they behold many wonders.
> The "Mr. Hyde" facet of Terry appears most mysteriously every Saturday night (10 P.M.) on WBKB's *Shock Theatre*. The sound of shattering glass and

clinking chains transform jovial Terry into a gleeful creature of darkness whose habitat is a dank candlelit cellar.

Terry's Mad Marvin is a smoldering fiend who delights in shocking his viewers by torturing an attractive young blonde whose face has been thus far obscured from sight.

But somehow Terry doesn't frighten his audience as much as he does himself. The all-consuming fear that gnaws at this "Jekyl-Hyde" [*sic*] personality is that his alter-ego may take control of him while hosting the younger sets [sic] favorite, *Jobblewocky Place.*

Although Terry Bennett's Marvin character never did take control over his "big brother" persona on his children's program, a kind of reversal of that possibility did occur one Saturday night on *Shock Theatre.* On that 1958 episode, with the week's movie segment ending and the Marvin break commencing, some viewers not familiar with *The Jobblewocky Place* must have been totally confused; because sitting on Marvin's lap, decked out in his own black turtleneck sweater and sport jacket, was a rather perplexed Red Flannels.

To viewers who had never seen or heard of *The Jobblewocky Place*, this must have been an *outré* image indeed. And it had to be even stranger to *Shock Theatre* fans who had no idea that Terry was a ventriloquist. Weirder yet was the moment Red began talking, while the guy upon whose lap he sat made him talk without moving his lips.

But strangest of all was when the dummy recited the mantra familiar to just about every kid living in Chicago whose family owned a TV set:

"Igglehocky, trobblebocky ... one ... two ... Jobblewocky!"

Definitely Not *a Fan*

By January of 1958, *Shock Theatre* had already become the most popular, highest-rated program on WBKB's local schedule. As noted that month by television critic Terry Turner in his article "What Fun to Shock 'Em," published in the *Chicago Daily News*, approximately 40 Marvin fan clubs had sprung into existence. Terry Bennett, now recognizable to the public wherever he went, even without the black outfit and disguising glasses, was constantly being stopped on the street by fans wanting his autograph.

As to the films he was running on *Shock Theatre*, Bennett told the other Terry, "I like horror movies. I guess it's the kid in me."

Although the vast majority of published letters about *Shock Theatre* were positive, and while Terry himself claimed to like the movies he was showing on the program, not everybody in Chicago felt the same way. One quite serious detractor would make his opinions and feelings about the show quite clear following the March 15 telecast of Universal's movie *Man Made Monster* (1941). The movie *Man Made Monster* starred Lon Chaney, Jr., in his first major horror role. He played "Dynamo Dan, the Electric Man," a likable young chap who, after surviving a bus accident during which everyone else on board was electrocuted, falls under the power of a mad electrical genius played by Lionel Atwill, a familiar face to fans of the *Shock!* package of films. As Dan has an unusual tolerance for electrical shock, Atwill's character uses him as a human guinea pig.

Via a series of increasingly strong dosages of electricity, the crazed scientist transforms McCormick into a glowing, virtually mindless engine of destruction, and forces him to kill. Condemned to die in the electric chair, Dan is only made more powerful by its charges. In the end, after inadvertently killing some more people, Dan, like so many other good 1940s monsters, destroys his creator, then perishes himself.

Man Made Monster was, in many ways, typical of the horror movies made during the '40s. No blood is shown, there are no severed limbs. Dan's experience in the electric chair and his subsequent killing of some prison guards occurs entirely off-screen, as if Universal was coyly anticipating possible censorship by the Breen Office.

Indeed, if *Man Made Monster* were made today, it might very well receive a "G" rating, acceptable for audiences of all ages.

Marvin introduced *Man Made Monster* with his usual flair:

> "Tonight's story is called *Man Made Monster*, the story of a mother-in-law. By now a lot of you assume that I don't like mothers-in-law. That's not true. I've always been pleasant to them, and *smile* ... as I bury them.
>
> "Tonight's story takes place far away. Which reminds me of the last time I had a vacation. The weather was miserable. All sunny and nice! But there's one thing I like about rain. I like to drive in the rain. Here's a picture of me driving one of those foreign cars. It was a beautiful...."

Marvin's introduction dissolved to the opening scene of *Man Made Monster*, showing a bus speeding through the rain and crashing into a high-voltage tower, an accident fatal to everyone inside save for Dan McCormick.

So far that second Saturday of March, all was happening on *Shock Theatre* as usual. But *Man Made Monster* was playing on a television show in Chicago, a city where censoring of movies was just "business as usual," i.e., trimming down movies — especially horror pictures and those showing nudity or partial nudity — for both theatrical and TV showings.

Oftentimes Windy City theatres ran horror movies intact, but restricted their audiences. One Chicago theatre, as late as 1956, had booked a triple bill of the Realart-reissued *Frankenstein* (advertised as "The Original Uncut Version"), *Murders in the Rue Morgue* and *WereWolf of London*, and branded their triple bill "Adults Only."

That same year a number of other Chicago neighborhood theatres would run, on an "Adults Only" basis, a double-bill of two British productions, *Chamber of Horrors* (1940) and *The Human Monster*. Both films would soon be shown — uncensored — on Chicago TV, the latter on *Shock Theatre*.

John Justin Smith, amatuer reporter employed by the *Chicago Daily News*, seemed offended by *Shock Theatre* in general and *Man Made Monster* in particular. In the article "They're Aimed at Teen-Age Audience: Shock Films: Good or Bad?" Smith offered his opinions and feelings about the program, its host and *Man Made Monster*. Readers could probably guess in what direction Smith's article might go, given the introduction preceding his text:

> John Justin Smith, a *Daily News* reporter, is the father of seven children. Television watching is something of a problem in his home because of the horror shows. Here he tells about his investigations of those shows.

Smith began presenting his "investigation" by reminding readers that, just a decade ago, many of Hollywood's horror flicks ("which make a dirty joke of death") "were stamped 'Adults Only' by the Chicago police censor board. This meant that "No youngster may see them legally in a Chicago theater.'"

The reporter noted that titles previously restricted to "Adults Only" audiences included *The Mummy's Hand* and *WereWolf of London*, both of which had already aired on *Shock Theatre*.

Smith's article included a comment by an unidentified police censor: "We can't touch those movies [shown on *Shock Theatre*]. Our jurisdiction covers theaters, not television." Smith seemed disturbed by an (again unidentified) 11-year-old boy's rather simplified summarization of how he recalled the plot of *Man Made Monster*, which the child had watched on *Shock Theatre*:

> "It was neat. First there's a bus wreck. Five guys got killed by electricity, but one guy lived.
> **"Then this guy goes to a scientist's house and they find out he's got fewer corpuscles and can stand electricity better than other people.**
> "So after a while they experiment and he kills the scientist. (By strangulation.)
> "Then when they put him in the electric chair the guy lights up like a light and he kills a few guards and the warden and escapes.
> "It was real neat then. The electric guy ... came to some people on a hay ride.
> **"He killed about 18 of them.**
> "He goes to the scientist's house and takes a beautiful girl and starts to run away with her.

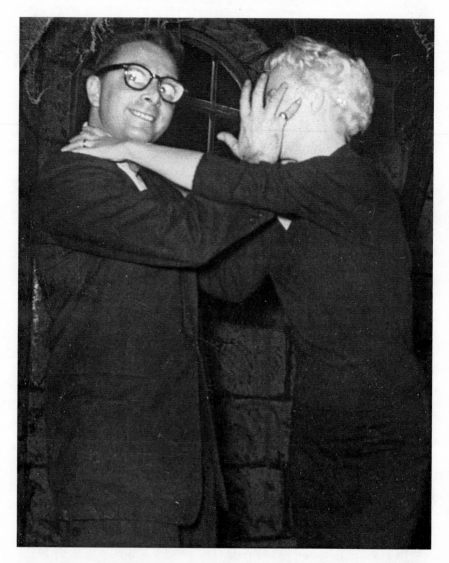

For once Dear (Joy Bennett) turns the tables on Marvin (Terry Bennett), in this gag photograph taken on the set of *Shock Theatre*.

"Dan walked into a barbed wire fence that punctured the rubber suit he was wearing. He drops the girl and when the wire hits him all his juice runs out and he dies."

On that happy note, the 11-year-old was supposed to go to bed.

Smith seemed to find Marvin, especially his popularity with young people, at least as distressing as the movies. The reporter pointed out that kids, many of them "only" in the seventh or eighth grade, tended to regard the *Shock Theatre* M.C. as "neat" or "a raid, a real raid." The reporter seemed particularly disturbed by Marvin's growing success:

> And Mad Marvin, it is reported, has been invited to discuss a series of shock music phonograph records with a record company.
>
> ... Marvin is expected to be a wow as a record salesman. Something in his field, a record called "Dinner with Drac" [performed by TV horror host John Zacherle, then still playing his Roland character in Philadelphia] has hit the best-seller lists.

The reporter further noted that some kids "**are sidelighting in cannabalism** [*sic*] **and vampirism.**"

And if Smith was put off by the storyline *of Man Made Monster,* he must have been even more distressed if he happened to watch *Shock Theatre* the night of the movie's showing. During the picture's fourth break, after "Dynamo Dan" is walked into the death house, Marvin, as always "neat" and "a real raid," tortured hapless Dear. Dear had been strapped to an electric chair; unlike Dan, however, she was not off-camera:

> Dear's body begins to quiver and smoke as the current crackles through it.
>
> "Well, our hero with the 100-plus body is really getting around. Isn't that right, Dear? What's the matter, Dear? Are you feeling warm?"
>
> Dear points toward an electric cord plugged into the wall.
>
> "Oh, your hair is sufficiently curled?" Marvin yanks out the cord, picks up Dear's hand and takes a little bite from her finger. "Don't complain! Now you're the toast of the town!"

Smith's article appears to have been mostly ignored by the people who read it. The show's ratings continued to climb.

Much of the show's increasing popularity in 1958, of course, can be credited to Joy Bennett's more developed characterization of Dear. The character was still being put through the same kinds of tortures that her predecessor had endured. Saturday upon Saturday Marvin hanged her, shot her, strangled her, poisoned her, stabbed her and blew her up, perpetrating whatever demises Bennett's crafty mind could devise.

And, like the Dear that came before her, Joy Bennett's version of the character always returned apparently no worse for wear.

8

Son of Shock!

Shock Theatre continued to show movies from Screen Gems' *Shock!* package into early 1958.

Unlike other local stations running the *Shock!* package, which tended to run all the movies including the crime melodramas, the Chicago version — either because of a decision by Terry Bennett or the WBKB brass — opted not to show all 52 offerings. Possibly, since a good number of the films in the *Shock!* package were not even borderline horror movies, those titles were not shown on Chicago's *Shock Theatre*. Perhaps viewers would have turned away from the show if subjected to movies about mundane murders, thefts and other crimes.

Titles from the Screen Gems package not shown on Chicago's *Shock Theatre* included *Secret of the Chateau, Enemy Agent, Destination Unknown, The Witness Vanishes, Nightmare, The Man Who Cried Wolf, Reported Missing, Dangerous Woman, The Spy Ring, Sealed Lips, The Last Warning, A Dangerous Game, Mystery of the White Room, Night Key* and *The Great Impersonation,*.

Some of these films, already purchased by WBKB, would not be wasted, however. For example, *Night Key*, in which the inventor (Boris Karloff) of a new kind of burglar alarm gets involved with criminals who use it for their own purposes, was shown instead on a weeknight.

The Great Impersonation may have been rejected outright by WBKB, even though that movie included a ghost subplot, a weird lunatic played by Dwight Frye (who had played the hunchbacked Fritz in *Frankenstein* and bug-eating Renfield in *Dracula*) and other horror-related trappings. Oddly, that movie turned up on rival Channel 2 at 11:30 P.M. on Saturday night, June 18, 1960, not long after *Shock Theatre* was canceled. The movie was shown on the CBS affiliate's new film series *Mystery Theater*, perhaps an attempt by the channel to claim the old *Shock Theatre* timeslot using a similar title.

Eliminating some of the movies from Screen Gems' total of 52 did, of course, leave vacancies that needed to be filled if *Shock Theatre* were to continue along on its weekly schedule. Eventually the show would have to resort to rerunning some movies, but that would not happen until January 3, 1959, with the second airing of *Dracula*.

Shock Theatre compensated for the unaired titles by showing movies that were not part of the Screen Gems collection. Fortunately, a number of other horror pictures were already catalogued in WBKB's film library. Some of these non-canonical titles were even superior in various ways to many of the old Universal films. These movies, made by 20th Century–Fox, RKO and Columbia, would nicely fill the slots left open by the rejected Universal titles.

On March 22, 1958, one week after *Man Made Monster*, *Shock Theatre* showed its first non–*Shock!* horror movie, *Dr. Renault's Secret* (1942), made by 20th Century–Fox. It was the story of yet another unorthodox scientist, this one portrayed by George Zucco, who, using a variety of techniques, evolves a gorilla (played by cowboy star Ray "Crash" Corrigan) into a somewhat "off" human being (character actor J. Carrol Naish) with the usual results.

Marvin began the March 22 show by, as usual, descending the cellar stairs. Dear was in the dungeon hooked up to a large console-like electrical machine (that would serve many purposes on the show, depending upon the needs of the skit), her body shaking from the zapping current.

"Oh, are you still here?" asks Marvin.

He pulls the machine's main switch, shutting it down. Released from the current, Dear falls, apparently electrocuted.

"Oh, Dear, I guess she's really falling for me. [*laughs*]. This is really quite a machine my neighbor gave me. It's quite good, but if used wrongly can be harmful and dangerous. Sometimes, for example, I could pull the wrong switch and we'd get a commercial."

Which Marvin does get, after which he continues....

"I guess I pulled the wrong switch. Tonight's story is *Dr. Renault's Secret*. I'll let you in on his secret. (In a whisper:) He's got bad breath."

Over the next year and more, *Shock Theatre* would continue to supplement its depleted *Shock!* list of films with other non–Universal horror movies. These titles included Bela Lugosi's *The Human Monster* (1940), a lurid and sometimes sadistic English-made adaptation of a story by Edgar Wallace; *The Son of Kong* (1933), an inferior sequel to the classic *King Kong*, about a giant ape on an island of prehistoric animals; *I Walked with a Zombie* (1943), a story about Voodoo and the walking dead; *The Body Snatcher* (1945) starring Karloff and Lugosi, a tale inspired by the real-life exploits of 19th century "resurrection men" Burke and Hare; and *The Brighton Strangler* (1945), in which an actor assumes the murderous traits of a character he had played on the stage; *The Undying Monster* (1942), a werewolf story involving a family curse; and *Hangover Square* (1945), a psychological thriller about a composer (Laird Cregar) compelled to commit murder.

More in line with the *Shock!* product were *The Return of the Vampire* and *Cry of the Werewolf,* both from Columbia Pictures in 1944 (see section below).

These movies fit well into *Shock Theatre*'s format; but soon there would be no need to make such substitutions. Additional product was about to come to WBKB by way of Screen Gems.

Son of Shock!

Early in 1958, Screen Gems, capitalizing on the successful sale of its first batch of horror movies to television stations, put together a sequel package. Echoing such titles as *Son of Frankenstein* and *Son of Dracula,* Screen Gems dubbed its new package *Son of Shock!*

As with its first package, Screen Gems sent out a set of 8 × 10 photographs representing each movie, and a promotional brochure describing the movies, (this publication was not as elaborate as the booklet issued to promote the original *Shock!* movies). WBKB, while still not having completely exhausted its cache of movies culled from Screen Gems' original 52, bought the new package.

Included in *Son of Shock!* were a number of Universal horror movies featuring some of the studio's top monsters, like *House of Frankenstein, The Mummy's Curse* and *Son of Dracula.* Possibly these and other titles had been reserved for the purpose of putting together a follow-up horror-movies package:

Son of Shock! comprised the following Universal titles:

Black Friday (1940)	*House of Dracula* (1945)
Bride of Frankenstein (1935)	*House of Frankenstein* (1944)
Captive Wild Woman (1943)	*The Invisible Man's Revenge* (1944)
The Ghost of Frankenstein (1942)	*The Mummy's Curse* (1944)

Added to the *Son of Shock!* package were some 1930s-1940s horrors made by Screen Gems' parent company Columbia Pictures, including the popular series of so-called "Mad Doctor" movies starring Boris Karloff:

Before I Hang (1940)	*Island of Doomed Men* (1940)
Behind the Mask (1932)	*The Man They Could Not Hang* (1939)
The Black Room (1935)	*The Man Who Lived Twice* (1936)
The Boogie Man Will Get You (1942)	*The Man with Nine Lives* (1940)
The Devil Commands (1941)	*Night of Terror* (1933)
The Face Behind the Mask (1941)	*The Soul of a Monster* (1944)

Cry of the Werewolf, also shown on *Shock Theatre,* was a horror film made by Columbia Pictures. It was released to Chicago TV prior to Screen Gems' *Shock!* or *Son of Shock!* film packages.

Columbia titles conspicuous by their absence were two of that studio's more "high profile" horror movies from of the '40s, *The Return of the Vampire*, an imitation Universal about a Dracula-like vampire (Bela Lugosi) and his werewolf slave, set in England during World War II, and *Cry of the Werewolf* (1944), the studio's not entirely successful answer to the moody horror product being produced by Val Lewton at RKO, about a young woman who inherits her gypsy mother's werewolf affliction. Actually, both of these films had already been made available to local television stations, and, as noted before, were two of the non–*Shock!* titles that Marvin had showed earlier in 1958.

Chicago's *Shock Theatre* did not show all 21 *Son of Shock!* motion pictures, either. This time the WBKB program eliminated the Boris Karloff-Peter Lorre comedy *The Boogie Man Will Get You*, reserving its showing for a weeknight.

The first movie from the *Son of Shock!* assortment shown on *Shock Theatre*, on the night of April 19, was the tepid Columbia programmer *The Soul of a Monster* (1944). It involved a deal made with the Devil through the supernatural powers of a beautiful woman. Given the date this show was aired, Marvin's opening words were timely.

Marvin descends the cellar stairs with his arms filled with papers. "Hello, I'm Marvin. I just finished filling out my income tax. Well, actually, I didn't do it. My neighbor upstairs did it. He's a CPA. A crooked public accountant! As a matter of fact, I was going to use 'Her' as a dependent, but I couldn't prove she was alive. My neighbor spent so much time working on my tax return that he didn't fill his own out. He doesn't care, though. He says he hasn't filled his return out correctly in 13 years."

Marvin reacts to sounds of police sirens, cars pulling up, police whistles, pistol shots and finally a body falling.

"Well, he won't have to fill his tax out next year either."

He walks over to Dear, who is sitting in a chair. "Did you fill out your form." She arises and strikes a sexy pose. "Yes," Marvin says, grinning, "I see!"

After the commercial....

"Tonight's story is called *The Soul of a Monster* and is taken from an original story written by Bugs Bunny. Not *the* Bugs Bunny. His cousin. You see, everybody writes stories nowadays. I wrote one too. Here it is," he says, holding up a sheet of paper. "For the benefit of those of you who suffer from near-sighted television screens, let's take a closer look...."

"The Ape Woman" and Her "Return"

Oddly, on two occasions *Shock Theatre* changed the titles of entries in the *Son of Shock!* package.

At 10 PM tonight, you will learn of the strange, diabolical spell that caused Dr. Winson to exchange his immortal soul for the price of life. See George Macready, Rose Hobart and Jim Bannon in THE SOUL OF A MONSTER – 10 PM TONIGHT on SHOCK THEATRE – WBKB Channel 7

The Soul of a Monster was the first selection from Screen Gems' *Son of Shock!* film package to be shown on *Shock Theatre.*

Univeral Pictures' last stab at creating a new series monster comprised three sequential movies featuring the character of Ape Woman Paula Dupree: *Captive Wild Woman* (1943) and *Jungle Woman* (1944), both with Acquanetta as the character, and *The Jungle Captive* (1945), with Vicky Lane in that role and also featuring Marvin's seeming favorite Rondo Hatton.

Like the earlier-shown *Dr. Renault's Secret*, the Ape Woman saga focused upon a gorilla (again, Ray Corrigan) transformed by a mad scientist (John Carradine) into a human, this time a beautiful young woman, with disastrous consequences. The middle Ape Woman movie *Jungle Woman*, perhaps for its shorter length, was not included in the *Son of Shock!* package.

By the time *Shock Theatre* showed "The Ape Woman" on June 6, 1959, Terry's "scripts"—at one time at least including all the words that Marvin would speak in every one of his appearances on a given show—had evolved into no more than very brief summaries of what he and the other performers on the show were supposed to do. The "script" (or, more accurately, the outline) for the opening action of the June 6 airing, following the first commercial, occupied less than three typewritten lines:

OPENING: Marv and Dear talking about Dear gaining weight ... reminds
Marv that tonight's story is called "The Ape Woman" ... gestures how easy
it is to resemble an ape ... (DISS TO FILM)

For some reason never revealed, possibly because the original titles may
have suggested jungle adventures in the Tarzan mold, *The Jungle Captive* and
Captive Wild Woman were shown on Chicago's *Shock Theatre* as "The Ape
Woman" and "Return of the Ape Woman," respectively. The new titles "kind
of" worked because the program didn't show the opening titles of its movies
anyway, going instead directly from Marvin's opening bits to the first scene.
Unfortunately *Shock Theatre* showed *The Jungle Captive*, the *third* movie in
the Ape Woman trilogy, *before* running *Captive Wild Woman*, the entry that
introduced the character. That meant that the movie run on *Shock Theatre* as
"The Ape Woman" was a *sequel* to the later-shown "Return of the Ape
Woman," which was, in actuality, the *original* film of that series. This mix-
up must have really confused viewers who tried making sense out of the already
loose continuity that existed from one Universal series movie to the next. In
the case of the Ape Woman movies, there was the added problem of not knowing the events that had unfolded in the middle entry *Jungle Woman!*

In 1960, as *Shock Theatre* continued to run movies following the Bennetts'
departure, in its very late-night timeslot, the two Ape Woman entries retained
their bogus titles. By that time, without Marvin to introduce the films, there
was no reason to bypass the opening credits, which some viewers who stayed
up late enough got to see for the first time. Nevertheless, the titles "The Ape
Woman" and "Return of the Ape Woman" were retained, simply written
crudely on cards set up before a TV camera.

Years later, when the Universal horror films continued to be shown on
local Chicago programs, like WGN's *Creature Features*, the Ape Woman
movies — all three of them — would play on television again, finally under
their correct titles

Continuing Through 1958

Shock Theatre was running in high gear; and while the weeks and months
passed, its format continued to expand. All the while the very talented Terry
Bennett was looking for new and more elaborate gimmicks and stunts to
enhance the show he created.

In the character's gradual evolution, Dear had become a bit more resourceful, not always requiring the services of Marvin to "do her in." This became
evident on May 10, 1958, when Marvin showed Universal's *The Invisible Man*

Returns (1940) starring a young Vincent Price in the title role. The Marvin and Dear sketch was staged after the penultimate break in the movie.

Marvin, trying to make Dear comfortable, offers her a cigarette. She takes it. He lights it for her and makes certain that she is nice and relaxed.

"I'll bet you're all waiting for me to do something to her, right?" he asks his viewers. "Well, I'm not."

To her, he says, "You're old enough now to do things yourself.

Dear nods, then starts choking herself.

"Now," says Marvin, "while you get a stranglehold on yourself, I'll choke up while watching our commercial...."

9

Shocking New Developments

Up through the spring of 1958, Marvin and Dear would carry on as usual with their macabre activities.

Marvin had been conducting some sinister experiment during the breaks in *The Mummy's Tomb*, a 1942 Universal Pictures sequel to the already shown *Mummy's Hand*.

Marvin, wearing a gas mask, and Dear are standing near the closed door of his laboratory.

"Well, anyway, now it's time for me to try my new experiment," Marvin tells Dear. "Now, Dear, this gas is very dangerous. That's why I'm wearing this mask ... and it's not because of our story tonight. Be sure and keep this door closed! The only way anyone could stand this gas is with a gas mask."

Marvin reaches for the doorknob. "Now I'm going in." He enters the lab, shutting the door behind him.

Curious as to what is happening in the lab, Dear peeks inside.

Marvin exits the lab and warns her, "I told you this gas is very poisonous. Keep the door closed!"

He returns to the lab and again Dear opens the door.

"Look, Dear," Marvin says, again stepping out of the lab, "you don't understand. The gas is poisonous. You could get very hurt. Here, let me show you."

Marvin pushes Dear into the laboratory, with the expected result.

"Imagine that...," he says, "I forgot to give her the gas mask!"

Marvin's on-and-off scientific experiments didn't always result in Dear's demise. On June 7, when *Shock Theatre* showed *Son of Dracula* (1943), Marvin's dabbling in his laboratory yielded a different kind of result. *Son of Dracula* had, via some impressive special effects executed by John P. Fulton, depicted the vampire Count Alucard's (Lon Chaney, Jr.) ability to transform into a bat. When the first break in the movie came around, Marvin was wondering if such a metamorphosis were actually possible.

Marvin browses through various books having titles like *How to Be a Vampire for Fun and Profit*, *What Every Vampire Should Know About People* and *Be Anemic and Still Be a Success*.

Dear looks over Marvin's shoulder, trying to see what he is reading.

He tells her, pointing at one of the pages, "There, Dear. I think I've found out how to turn you into a vampire." She laughs, skeptical. "Don't you believe it? Here...." Marvin gets a glass containing a liquid and hands it to Dear. "Drink this. You'll see what I mean."

Dear drinks the concoction and vanishes; and the shadow of a bat is cast on the wall.

"See, Dear," says an excited Marvin, "it worked! You've finally got that fur coat you wanted. Now I'll turn you back again. What pages was that on...?" He starts paging through the book as the bat's shadow remains on the wall.

"I could have sworn it was in here somewhere...."

There would be a considerable amount of very *real* experimentation done on *Shock Theatre* in 1958, none of it having to do with Marvin's fictional mad lab, most of it involving the show's characters. For example, as Dear's character continued to evolve, she became more proactive and less a faceless prop or victim, replacing her light-colored garb with a black dress in the process.

Shorty and Orville

Weird new characters began to be introduced to the dungeon set, not all of them portrayed by human actors (thus not having to be paid).

There was a talking skull named Mr. Bones — in reality a hollow rubber skull, made by Lou Tannen's Magic Store in New York, but purchased by Bruce Newton from the Treasure Chest. By inserting a hand through an opening in the back of the skull, the mouth could be made to open and close. Terry Bennett's ventriloquial abilities supplied Mr. Bones' voice.

There was also the Glob, a shiny gelatinous mas inspired by the then-current science fiction movie hit *The Blob*. The Glob did absolutely nothing but lie in its container.

But the two most significant character additions were played by human performers — a hulking Frankenstein Monster called Shorty and a grotesque hunchback named Orville. As Kerry Bennett explained to the author, "My Mom said that my Dad never wanted the show to get stale, so as time went on, he brought in new faces like Orville and Shorty, both staff members who were utilized for the show."

Shorty, called "Franky" or "Frankenstein" in his earlier appearances on the show, was essentially the Frankenstein Monster. Fortunately for WBKB, no search was required to find someone to fill that role. There was already a person on the Channel 7 payroll who met the physical requirements for such a sizable character. As a staffer, he was already doing several shows a day and functioning in multiple capacities. Now he would have one more assignment.

Bruce Newton was a WBKB staff employee, and the station's staffers did as they were told. Thus, a request made to Newton by the station's higher-ups was not one he could refuse (although he tried his best). Newton told Okuda and Yurkiw in their book *Chicago TV Horror Movie Shows*:

> One day Red Quinlan came to me and said, "You're going to be Frankenstein on *Shock Theatre* next Saturday night." I said, "No, I'm not." I was making a nice salary, but I was already putting in long hours six days a week and I didn't feel like giving up my Saturday nights. So Red said, "You'll do it or you're fired." Then I said, "In that case, I'll be very glad to do it." [laughs]

With the extra height provided by high-soled boots he wore as Shorty, Newton stood about seven feet tall. But since WBKB refused to pay additional wages for another speaking role, the only sounds Shorty would vocalize were grunts, snarls and growls, uttered while Newton gestured with his hands and arms. Interviewed by Rick Thomas, Newton stated, "My costume — coat, pants, mask. The makeup person originally put putty on my face, which did work well but took a long time."

Inevitably this makeup, which (as Newton told Okuda and Yurkiw) took approximately 90 minutes to apply, was abandoned, probably serving no purpose other than a test. By the time Newton actually appeared on camera as the character, he'd opted for a method of becoming the Frankenstein Monster character that was more practical, comfortable (albeit not under the studio lights) and less time-consuming. It was done as it *had* been done the previous year, when he and his WBKB colleagues made their personal appearances as monsters to promote *Shock Theatre*: Newton slipped on a Don Post Franken-stein Monster rubber mask to which fake hair was attached. Most likely this was the same mask that Newton had worn when he his monstrous cohorts stalked the animal cages at the zoo and the halls of the museum.

Orville was Marvin's unsightly hump-backed servant character, played by Ronny Born. Like Newton, Born was a WBKB staff performer and, as such, was told that he *had* to play the Orville character, *period*. Unlike Joy Bennett, Born got to speak real words on the show, although much of his dia-logue consisted of "Yes, master" or "No, master."

Born told the author how he was cast:

> I was working at WBKB doing the puppet voices for *Princess Mary's Castle*. [Terry Bennett] needed a supporting cast. He [used] Joy as "Dear," who never talked but did a lot of screaming. You never saw her face which was a shame because she was very pretty. Rounding out the cast was Bruce Newton, a big tall fellow who worked with me on the Princess Mary show; he would be "Shorty," a Frankenstein character who plodded his way through life but unfortunately, or fortunately depending on your taste in voices, also didn't speak. [It was decided

that] it would be nice to have someone on the show that Terry could converse with in more than grunts, so why not me? I had all the qualifications. So they asked me to be on the show. I was delighted. So Terry and I created the bent-over one-eyed character known as Orville.

While Born was fortunate in being able to work steadily at Channel 7, his luck often soured when it came to Orville's appearance. Much like the senior Lon Chaney in his silent-movie version of *The Hunchback of Notre Dame*, Born was required to enact his role in an uncomfortable crouching, bent-over position.

Equally unpleasant

Ronny Born, mainly a voice-over actor at WBKB, played *Shock Theatre*'s Orville, a grotesque but lovable hunchbacked character (courtesy Terry Tiz).

for Born, his face was heavily made-up with, presumably, nose-putty affixed to his skin with spirit gum. The guise included a bulging artificial eye. The make-up was quite elaborate for a local TV show and time-consuming to apply. As he explained to the author:

> The only drawback was the make-up and the fact that it took up all Saturday night. In those days everything was performed live, so I would come in allowing a whole hour to apply the make-up, which consisted of one eye being covered and inserting a contact lens in the other, so I could read the cue card. (Remember, Terry and I had the only speaking roles, the others were able to ad-lib their assorted grunts, groans and screams.)
> By the way, I did my own make-up. I would sit with one eye closed, heavy make-up running down my face, looking like a Cyclops, practicing my English accent for three hours ... but what the hell, that's show biz.

Unfortunately the putty tended to melt under the hot studio lights, sometimes literally falling off Born's face — on camera and in close-up — before the show's end. But such problems rarely stopped *Shock Theatre*'s live cameras from capturing the action.

But, make-up mishaps notwithstanding, at least Born got to speak on the show. As he related to the author:

> I was known as a man with a thousand voices all sounding the same, but I only needed one. So I did a voice that was a cross between Winston Churchill and Groucho Marx. Anyway, Terry liked it and he ran the show. And the best part of me was that they didn't have to pay me a cent, since I was on staff, and this was only once a week and wouldn't interfere with my main job — which was *Princess Mary's Castle*. So, I eagerly took the added role and agreed to the raise which was "zero."

A typical skits involving Dear, Shorty and Orville was this one, performed on March 7, 1959, the night that *Shock Theatre* showed the *Son of Shock!* movie *The Ghost of Frankenstein* (1942), in which the Monster, now portrayed by Lon Chaney, Jr., is given a new brain.

By the first break in the film, Marvin had already explained how proud Shorty was that night — because he was the star of the movie.

> Marvin says that it's time that he, Dear, Shorty, and Orville make a movie of their own. Marvin will direct, Dear and Shorty will be its stars, and Orville, despite his bad eye, will be the cameraman.
>
> And Marvin has the greatest idea for a movie — filming an actual death!
>
> No big surprise, Dear is to be the star of that scene.
>
> Dear is afraid. She doesn't want to die. But when Marvin explains how this movie will make her a big star with her name up in lights, she reconsiders.
>
> With Orville behind the movie camera, Marvin calls "Action!" and Shorty goes into his performance — strangling Dear. She falls and Marvin raves about how wonderful the scene went. Unfortunately, nobody had loaded film into the camera.
>
> "That's too bad," Marvin says, shrugging his shoulders. "If only there was film in the camera, she could have been the world's greatest actress."

In the second break, Dear was back, alive and well as always. Marvin, now holding a revolver, was still intent on filming a death scene, but this time he would take precautions:

> Marvin fires his gun to get everyone's attention.
>
> Dear is still frightened, but Marvin explains that, at the moment her death is to occur, a double will be substituted. In fact, Dear won't even be hurt. Again, reluctantly, Dear agrees to do the scene.
>
> While Orville lines up the scene through his movie camera, Marvin explains the action to Shorty and Dear: Shorty will stalk up to Dear and then slit her throat. But before Shorty's knife can cause Dear any harm, Marvin will stop the action and Dear's double will step in.
>
> At least, that is Marvin's plan.

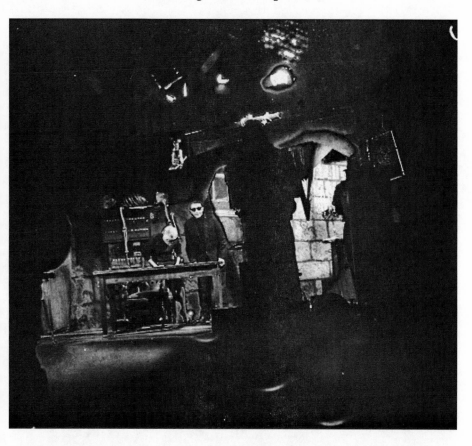

Behind-the-scenes look as Marvin (Terry Bennett) and Dear (Joy Bennett, now wearing her new black attire) enact a *Shock Theatre* skit during one of the breaks in a movie (courtesy Terry Tiz).

Marvin yells, "Roll it!" and Orville starts grinding away with his camera. With Marvin giving direction through a megaphone, Shorty lumbers up to Dear, knife in hand.

Marvin yells, "Cut!"

Which Shorty obediently does, slitting Dear's throat.

"I can't understand it," wonders Marvin. "Disney did it and won an Oscar."

The new additions to *Shock Theatre* did not go unnoticed by the press. Judy Kempski, in a 1958 newspaper article titled "Monsters Accompany Popular Personality in Cellar 'Haunt of Late Horror Program,'" wrote:

Amid the groans of hapless victims and the clanging of iron chains, comes the unique personality who hosts the popular Saturday night horror show, *Shock Theatre.*

In the eerie setting of an old haunted house cellar, Terry Bennett, known to millions as the diabolical and scatterbrained "Marvin," clowns with two of his monster friends and the masked girl, his wife. Explaining the reasons for the mask, Mr. Bennett says, "... it's just a gimmick to keep people guessing and also watching."

Basil?

There were also alterations pertaining to Marvin himself made in 1958.

Originally, as on the premiere episode of the program, Marvin spoke in a rather mild, soft-spoken voice, although he occasionally broke out into short

Terry Bennett, now sporting more comfortable dark glasses instead of the originals with the magnifying lenses, on the set of *Shock Theatre*. With the new spectacles, Terry could actually see his way around the set (courtesy Terry Tiz).

fits of maniacal laughter. Gradually, however, Marvin's voice began to change, getting louder, becoming higher in pitch, even shrill, with his crazy laugh heard more frequently.

Marvin's demeanor changed too, becoming less "laid back" and more hyperactively animated. Possibly these changes were simply a natural evolution of the character over time. However, as Terry's other show *The Jobblewocky Place* was so popular, he may have deliberately revised his Marvin persona in an attempt to separate it from the one that children were enjoying on weekday mornings.

Marvin's glasses changed too. The original thick-lensed spectacles that magnified his eyes to ridiculous proportions made actually seeing through them nearly impossible, forcing Terry to almost blindly feel his way around the set. By 1959 those trademark specs were gone, Marvin now sporting a pair of sunglasses. The "shades" were actually more in keeping with his beatnik image anyway.

But one truly shocking change pertaining to Marvin happened in the fall of 1958.

Rumors had begun to circulate suggesting that Terry might be leaving the show. Reinforcing these rumors, Marvin, near the end of one fall airing, told viewers that he was leaving *Shock Theatre*— going to Transylvania to visit his mysterious cousin Basil (pronounced "Bay-zil." with a long "a"). Viewers who loved the Marvin character were genuinely concerned. Was this announcement "for real" and, if so, would his departure be permanent?

The week that followed was a long one for true *Shock Theatre* fans, wondering what to expect next Saturday night.

Next week's show aired with Marvin nowhere to be seen. The program did, however, have a host. For while Marvin was supposedly off gallivanting somewhere in the wilds of Transylvania, the person he had left to visit came walking down those familiar dungeon stairs!

When Basil appeared with no Marvin in sight (at least in *plain* view), fans were braced for the worst; and that's exactly what some of them got. The complete opposite of Marvin, Basil was an overly couth, way too sophisticated, rather stuffy and arrogant aristocratic type. He was impeccably attired, in a dapper European-style suit complete with gloves and bowler hat. He carried a walking stick that he brandished as a potential weapon.

It wasn't just the way Basil dressed that made him such a contrast to Marvin. His countenance was very pale, with dark lines and deep circles around his eyes; and he spoke with a kind of stilted Bela Lugosi–style accent.

Adding insult to injury, Basil, upon seeing a 16 × 20" portrait of Marvin on the wall, turned it around — revealing, to his chagrin (and the viewers'

Ronny Born (Orville), Bruce Newton (Shorty), Joy Bennett (Dear) and Terry Bennett (Marvin) discuss an upcoming *Shock Theatre* skit (courtesy Bruce Newton).

surprise), a picture of Marvin as seen from the back. Perhaps that was an omen or foreshadowing or suggestion that Marvin had not departed forever? Marvin's fans could only hope....

Hope was there for those keen-eyed fans who cared to look *through* the thick clown-white make-up and black shading. Were they, in fact, perceiving glimpses of the familiar visage of Terry Bennett through the features of Basil?

Taken as his own character, there was nothing inherently wrong with Basil. He was a perfectly acceptable horror host.

As TV horror hosts went (and are still going), Basil was indeed an impressive and imposing character, both in his appearance and the way he was presented. His character was well defined and his patter perfectly timed for best comedic effect. Also, as most viewers probably guessed eventually, underneath this character calling himself by a new name was still the very talented and charismatic Terry Bennett.

He's Back!

When compared to Marvin, however, Basil fell short, lacking the original character's ghoulish glee and, dare it be stated, warmth. Kerry Bennett said the following about Basil:

> After speaking with my mom, it really appears that Basil was just my Dad throwing a curve ball at the show. I heard him do a similar thing here in Florida on the radio, as he would play fake radio guests live on the air.

Terry's "curve ball" clearly had a powerful effect. Viewers, almost all of them ardent Marvin fans, disliked his replacement–Basil's look, his clothes, arrogance, manner of speech, pretty much everything about him. They must have voiced their feelings in letters, phone calls, whatever; because after just a few weeks with Basil hosting the program, Marvin––happy, exuberant and sadistic as ever–made his triumphant return.

The movie for that night of October 4 was *I Walked with a Zombie*, another non–Screen Gems chiller. But to ardent Marvin fans the zombie film could hardly match in importance what would occur that night on the dungeon set. *Shock Theatre* fans were in for a joyous surprise.

The show opened as always, with someone coming down the stairs, at first seen only in shadow. This time, however, the shadow did not belong to Basil.

> Marvin greets his viewers, then goes to Dear, wondering if she will still recognize him after his temporary absence.
>
> Dear screams and faints.
>
> "Yep," says Marvin, "she remembers me."
>
> He looks around the place, spotting his picture hanging on the wall facing backwards. Turning the picture around, he quips, "You haven't changed a bit, you devil, you!"
>
> After the commercial, Marvin walks up to Dear, who is now sitting in a chair. "Well, Dear, I'm back. Did you miss me? It was nice in Transylvania. But Basil wasn't there like he said he'd be."
>
> He notices a pair of gloves on the table.
>
> "Oh, are these yours?" Marvin asks the woman. Dear mumbles, letting him know that the gloves aren't hers. Surprised, Marvin replies, "They're Basil's gloves? You mean Basil was here?"
>
> Marvin slips on the gloves and starts choking Dear, who begins to scream. "How could he do this to me ... how could he do this to me ... how could he...? Oh, stop screaming. With these gloves I leave no tell-tale stains."

Marvin was back, presumably for good; but the announcement he made at the end of that particular episode of *Shock Theatre* constituted fantastic news for fans of the show. Next week, Marvin said excitedly, something new would be added to the show — something he called a "shocktail party."

10

Shocktails and Shock Tales

On Saturday, December 6, 1958, one year after the debut of *Shock Theatre* on Chicago television, Terry, Joy and the rest of the cast and crew celebrated by having an in-studio anniversary party, complete with cake.

That year had been one of many changes *Shock Theatre*, especially during the fall and winter months.

Marvin — as early as the first telecast — had mentioned "shocktail parties," and after just a few mentions by Marvin of these fictitious affairs, they became a popular reality.

What was a "shocktail party"?

Presumably, in the beginning anyway, they were social events attended either by Marvin himself in the program's mini-universe between broadcasts, or they were actual parties thrown in the "real world," where fans gathered, sometimes dressed like Marvin, and serving drinks like Bloody Marys. Some of these gatherings were probably held on Saturday nights, allowing the guests to watch *Shock Theatre* on the host's television set while they partied.

Yet as *Shock Theatre* became more and more popular, the "shocktail party" also became something more ... considerably more.

By late 1958 it seemed to the WBKB executives that viewers simply could not get enough of *Shock Theatre*, Marvin and Dear. The powers-that-be made the decision to expand and also enrich their weekly hit.

On October 11, 1958, *Shock Theatre* ran its only movie made after the 1940s, and probably the worst film it ever showed, *Bride of the Monster*. But the movie itself was not the highlight of the evening.

That night WBKB augmented *Shock Theatre* to two hours. The new extension of *Shock Theatre* would commence at 11:30, right after the scheduled movie ended, thereby eliminating *Star Tonight*, a filmed dramatic anthology series with Hollywood movie stars. The new addition, which would soon be listed as its own separate program in some TV program guides, was appropriately named *Shocktail Party.*

Fans were elated, knowing that they would be treated each week to an extra 30 minutes of Marvin, Dear, Shorty and Orville. Viewers who tuned in for the first telecast got a *lot* more than they'd expected.

One significant change was a bigger set, revealing more of Marvin's dungeon. But more — and better — surprises were to come.

Downbeat for Deadbeats

The biggest (and, to many fans, best) addition came in the form of six musicians. The half-hour extension was, after all, supposed to be a *party*—and parties have music.

It may have been Terry Bennett who suggested that *Shocktail Party* have its own band, possibly a first for any show running the *Shock!* movie package. But Terry wasn't interested in just *any* band or some novelty group. He wanted his *Shocktail Party* band to be the *very best* that WBKB could afford.

Terry's wish was granted! And he didn't need to look far to find and collect his musicians.

Enter, the Deadbeats (sometimes spelled in print as the variants "Dead Beats," "Dead-Beats," or "Marvin's Dead Beats").

The individual musicians had been hired by Rex Maupin, the head of the station's musical staff. As explained to me by Terry Tiz, back in the *Shock Theatre* days (and still today) president of the "Dead-Beats Fan Club":

> ABC/WBKB contracted only the highest skilled musicians. Back in those days, Chicago was a prime location for the music industry. Many albums, commercials, etc., were produced and recorded in the Windy City. Being contracted to the station meant all the lucrative studio sessions and gigs would be taboo, but there was that steady paycheck and guaranteed work.
>
> It was not easy to become a staff musician. There was an audition process. Musicians must read music, play any style required, perform for specific lengths of time, and stop when a station break was required. And of course, the musician must play impeccably.

Chicago musicians were required to join Local 10, the city's branch of the American Federation of Musicians (the A.F. of M.), headed by James Petrello. The very powerful union boss had dictated to Chicago's local television stations the number of musicians they needed to maintain on staff whether they actually played or not.

The work a union musician was assured of getting every week as a WBKB

Marvin's Deadbeats, a band assembled from WBKB staff musicians and led by Sam Porfirio (accordion), brought a true coffeehouse mood to the *Shocktail Party* experience. Also in the photograph: (from left to right) Lenny Druss (clarinet), Russell Crandall (flute), Clay Campbell (drums), Harold Siegel (string bass) and (foreground) Patrick Ferreri (guitar).

staff musician was steady and well-paying; but such security — even for such an unpredictable career — had its down sides. There was no overtime money for extra work, even when the work hours were overly long, day and night. Moreover, playing music for the station proved to be a rather exclusive and therefore limiting gig.

As Tiz further explained to me:

> Back in those olden days, contracts were most beneficial to the company, not the talent. So the company could fire them, sorry "release" them with some notice. The musicians generally couldn't say "I quit." So the boys played the shows required....When the 30-minute *Shocktail Party* was added to the live Sat-

urday night broadcast, ABC had to get the A.F. of M.'s permission to have the band work a six-day week (at no extra pay).

Six musicians from a list of about 40 on the WBKB payroll were selected to comprise Marvin's "Deadbeats" (as the band was named), all of them top-of-the-line performers contracted to work only for that station or its network parent company ABC.

Before becoming Deadbeats, these musicians had already comprised a sextet working together in keyboard man Sam Porfirio's combo, a band that furnished music for a variety of WBKB programs including the children's shows *Here's Geraldine* and *Chatter's World*; the musical *Polka-Go-Round*; *Bob and Kay,* an early talk show starring local celebrities Bob Murphy and Kay Westfall; and *Playboy After Dark,* hosted by Chicago resident and *Playboy* founder-publisher editor Hugh Hefner.

The Deadbeats' membership consisted of group leader Porfirio (accordion, piano, anything with a keyboard), Russell Crandall (harp, some percussion), Harold Siegel (string bass), Patrick Ferreri (guitar, banjo), Lenny Druss (woodwinds, brass) and Clay Campbell (drums).

Ferreri told Okuda and Yurkiw in *Chicago TV Horror Movie Shows: From Shock Theatre to Svengoolie*:

> I was in the band for Don McNeill's *Breakfast Club* for nine years. Rex Maupin was the chief director of musical operations at WBKB. He was from the old school of radio; he had worked on radio shows like *Suspense* and wrote all the appropriate mood music. He could write any kind of music that was needed.
>
> One day, Rex said, "Pat, I've got bad news for you. You're going down to the TV station and you're going to wear funny costumes and do some funny things." Now, that's not exactly what I wanted to hear, and he knew it, but I did it out of respect for him. He was a world-class musician who just happened to be stuck in this chief director's position. I would have beat my brains out to make him happy — the other musicians felt that way, too, which is why we all agreed to do the show.

Clad in beatnik-black like Marvin, their faces covered in pasty-white make-up with black trimming, the group resembled zombies or maybe vampires. Their appearance as well as their musical abilities was simply perfect for *Shocktail Party.*

The Shows Go On

Usually the Deadbeats played behind music stands (designed by Frank Oakley to resemble tombstones) bearing the words "Marvin's Dead Beats."

Depending upon what Terry had devised for *Shocktail Party* on a particular night, the combo provided some really fine mood music, offering such appropriately Terry Bennett–named numbers as "Lullaby to Die For," "Cremation Concerto" and "Music for Murder."

At times the Deadbeats sang, too, generally in a listless, monotone style: The main vocals were mostly handled by Porfirio, Druss and Campbell, sometimes in a boisterous style bordering upon opera.

The band did a lot of standards having titles, themes or lyrics that fit well with the sinister yet humorous mood of *Shocktail Party*: "Witchcraft," "Taboo," "Mack the Knife." Excellent musicians, the Deadbeats could — and often did — play any style of music imaginable. They could imitate just about any other band in existence, usually adding to such impersonations the Deadbeats' own ghoulish spin.

They did spot-on parodies of well-known tunes (*e.g.,* "Ghoul Days," "Six Foot Under," "Ghoul Land Band-Aid" and "I Ain't Got No Body"), their lyrics having been rewritten by Terry. They also did entirely original numbers written specifically for the show, including the clever "Dear."

Sometimes the group brilliantly "twisted" the music they played, intentionally going off key or changing a number's timing. But no matter how they distorted a piece of music, the Deadbeats remained in complete control and knew exactly what they were doing. What they did wrong always came out totally correct.

In short, *Shock Theatre* and *Shocktail Party* lucked out in having just about the best house band in town, let alone the finest musicians working for WBKB.

Not Just Musicians

On occasion the Deadbeats participated in some of *Shocktail Party*'s skits. As Patrick Ferreri related to Okuda and Yurkiw in their book on Chicago television's horror hosts:

> Everyone connected with the show was cooperative, and even though most of us weren't really comedians, we did make an effort to make people laugh. Terry and Joy were a lot of fun to work with, and we did some pretty weird stuff. One time, I was sitting on the end of a teeter-totter, playing my electric guitar, and Sam Porfirio was on the other end, playing his accordion. I had to be careful to make sure the cord of my guitar was the right length, so I wouldn't get yanked off the teeter-totter when I went up in the air.
>
> Another time, there was a huge bucket of water on the set. The bucket had a hole in it so Terry could put on a rubber glove and stick his hand through the

The Deadbeats — from left to right, Sam Porfirio (accordion), Lenny Druss (clarinet), Russell Crandall (harp), Clay Campbell (drums), Harold Siegel (string bass) and (foreground) Patrick Ferreri (guitar) — in a *Shocktail Party* segment.

hole. The idea was that Joy would go bobbing for apples and, when she leaned into the bucket, Terry's arm would grab her. Well, while they were performing this bit live on the air, the bucket broke and all this water poured all over the set. I was worried I'd be electrocuted because of my electric guitar. What a mess — the station had to cut back to the movie *real* fast.

Among the Deadbeats' more fondly remembered accomplishments is their catchy instrumental signature music "Shocktail Theme," composed by Porfirio, that opened and closed each show. As a testimony to the musicians' talent and versatility, the piece never sounded quite the same twice. Sometimes (but not always) the theme would slyly segue into a couple familiar measures of Frédéric François Chopin's "Funeral March." The group performed their theme song at the beginning and end of the program, with dead-pan expressions, the result being hilarious.

Marvin and Dear often performed with the Deadbeats, although not as part of the band, doing parodies of popular songs. In one such performance, the duo did their unique version of a then-current Top 40 novelty hit "Kookie, Kookie, Lend Me Your Comb," written by Irving Taylor, with Terry mimicking the original number's Edd "Kookie" Byrnes and Joy doing Connie Stevens. Unlike Stevens, however, Joy made sounds vaguely suggesting some of the lyrics of the original song, substituting "Marvin"—actually something more like "Mah-whi"—for "Kookie."

Sometimes, backed by the Deadbeats' music (and Dear's vocal sounds), Marvin read letters purportedly sent in by viewers, like this one from an "anonymous" Joliet, Illinois, viewer:

> Dear Marvin,
> My husband takes me down to the basement every evening to help him with his woodwork. You see, he nails me to the inside of a box, and then closes the lid, and I nearly suffocate. Now he's talking about sawing off my limb for a lamp stand. What should I do?

Marvin's reply was simple:

> "Encourage him. Everyone should have a hobby."

Marvin, usually with Dear participating, also did parodies of currently popular television shows like *Peter Gunn* ("Marvin Musket"), *The Mickey Mouse Club*, *Dragnet* and *Alfred Hitchcock Presents*, always backed up by the Deadbeats' recreations of those programs' music themes.

With so much activity squeezed into each episode, *Shocktail Party* had become, in essence, a half-hour live variety show. When taking into account the fact that it followed a show already 90 minutes in length, and one requiring its own comedy skits and live Deadbeats music, the end result was truly amazing. Even more astonishing, the show was largely the responsibility of a man who already had an enormous workload, putting together and performing as himself—along with a collection of other characters—five days a week, an hour each day, on his morning children's show.

Still, Terry and his talented and loyal cast and crew made *Shocktail Party* happen.

Terry Tiz, who often visited the *Shock Theatre* set where he got to know the Deadbeats, recalled:

> Preparation for a *Shock Theatre* broadcast was straightforward. During the week the boys would rehearse each day after the morning kids' shows. Rehearsal would include songs that would be coming up that week. These might require the show's "talent" if required. New arrangements might be tested. On Saturday, they'd come in early evening, rehearse. There would be a tech rehearsal on set. Basic run-through, after which it was time for make-up and costumes.

The new no-movie format meant that Terry had the opportunity to experiment further. Even with the Deadbeats able to fill some of the air time with their music, the skits involving Marvin, Dear, Shorty and Orville could now be longer and more involved.

"Happy Harry" and Remotes

One of the new features Terry devised for *Shocktail Party* was the "Happy Harry" television commercial spoof.

The first of these phony commercials typified the ones yet to come. The *faux* TV ad was constructed over the final climactic act of the movie *Frankenstein*, wherein irate townspeople pursue the Frankenstein Monster with torches and trap him inside a windmill.

As "Happy Harry," Terry Bennett (wearing lighter-colored clothes and recalling the commercials he'd done himself for local retail chains like Polk Bros.) dubbed in his own voice. As the commercial's narrator, Terry assumed the persona of a clichéd, loud-mouthed, hard-selling announcer hawking some product (like "Happy Harry's Coffins"). Always, Marvin's patter was delivered over appropriate Deadbeats background music. Brilliantly Terry managed to insert his own original lines over dialogue spoken by the individual actors seen in the *Frankenstein* clip, never missing a beat.

That first "Happy Harry" proved to be a hit and fans loved Terry's latest accomplishment.

Audience response was encouraging. WBKB had a library-full of movies from which Terry could extract scenes, and not necessarily just horror titles. The station also had on hand its share of documentaries and old newsreel footage. Importantly, these fake advertisements devoured at least several minutes of air time, helping to help fill out *Shocktail Party*'s 30 minutes.

Another new feature was the remote camera segment, which gave the *Shock Theatre* performers a chance to get outside of the cramped WBKB studio. As Joy Bennett told Rick Thomas in *Filmfax* magazine, "We had a lot of latitude in those days and could pretty well call our own shots. Terry had a very creative mind, and therefore could think up various situations, and Red Quinlan allowed Terry to do various remotes."

The *Shocktail Party* remotes were shot on 16mm film. The segments were edited and then run on the show, with Marvin and an indecipherable Joy, cooing and uttering other sounds from behind her frilly mask, making funny comments over the silently shown filmed footage.

In one of these remotes, Marvin and Dear crashed Wrigley Field, home of the Cubs, Chicago's beloved baseball team. Once inside the stadium the two stars performed a series of visual gags, causing havoc on the playing field and interacting with the team. Marvin stole a base (literally), almost knocked himself out while swinging a bat (not the vampire kind) and performed other comedy gags. Joy told Thomas that the Chicago Cubs "were very cooperative in playing their roles." This remote ended with Marvin and Dear being ejected from the stadium.

Another filmed remote took Marvin and Dear to Lincoln Park Zoo, where they reacted in comical ways to the animals, surprised visitors who had just expected to see lions, bears and elephants that day, and performed other comedy bits.

Terry's Terror Tomes

One addition to the *Shocktail Party* was something new — and probably very surprising to the majority of viewers. This was the feature, again introduced by Terry Bennett, that he dubbed the "Shock Tale."

Terry's past skits and bits of business on *Shock Theatre* and *Shocktail Party* were intended to provide his audience with laughs — but the "Shock Tales" were designed to *scare* his viewers ... and *really* scare them!

The "Shock Tales" were dramatic, first-person readings, devoid of even a modicum of humor. And they allowed Terry to indulge at much higher levels both his writing and serious acting abilities, showing off his non-comedic creative chops.

These readings were done with only Marvin on camera, usually sitting down and seen in tight close-up. The material read was always horrific. The "Shock Tales" also differed from the usual *Shock Theatre* and *Shocktail Party* fare in yet another way: They were fully scripted by Terry.

One "Shock Tale" was described by an uncredited reporter in a late 1958 *Chicago Sun-Times* article with the headline "'Shocktale' Parties to Scare You to Death":

> For one of these readings he was going to take poison and relate to the audience how it felt to experience death. An antidote was on hand which, taken at the moment of death, would bring him back to life.
>
> Painfully, Bennett described his sensations after swallowing the fake poison; he told of dizziness, constriction in his chest. Then, writing in agony, he lurched for the antidote and knocked it on the floor.
>
> "That was pretty effective," Bennett said. "We got hundreds of letters about it."

Actually, Marvin's enactment of a dying man involved a lot more, as hallucinations and guilt drove the character he was playing deeper into despair, oblivion and madness to the accompaniment of eerie music and sound effects:

Why, I feel exhilarated. My body is growing lighter ... lighter.... I'm drifting like some fleeing cloud. And there's a bright light coming toward me ... coming closer ... closer ... closer ... it's too bright, it hurts. Oh, it's hurting my eyes ... my eyes ... it's beginning to blind me ... it's blinding ... blinding ... no, no, take it away ... it pains ... it hurts ... it's torturing ... ahhhhh! Now it's gone....

But I can't see. It's dark. I'm blind ... I'm blind ... those swishing noises ... wish ... swish ... I can't see them ... swish ... back and forth.... No, stop, I say!

Black feathers ... hard, mean black feathers.... I know they are black.... Now they are closing in ... in ... beating me on my body ... beating me ... closing in, wrapping around me, feathers ... wings ... black, hard, wrapping themselves around me.

Oh, now they are gone ... now ... lights.... I can see lights ... little lights coming closer ... closer ... millions of them. No, they are eyes ... staring eyes ... just eyes that leer and stare. Go away, eyes, go away.

What's that? No ... no ... no, I say. I don't want to see him. Yes, I remember.... Please, eyes. I don't want to see him. Yes ... yes, I cut him up. I cut him and cut him, yes ... yes.... I know I did ... each little piece I threw in the fire. Please, please, eyes, I don't want to see him. Oh, thank you, eyes ... he's fading ...fading....

Please, eyes, go away! No ... no ... not that, eyes ... not my father. No, please.... Yes, he was an old man. I wanted to see the bubbles. Please, eyes, I only wanted to see the bubbles. I pushed and pushed and his head went into the water and then the bubbles came. Oh, those beautiful bubbles! Wonderful light bubbles.

Please, eyes, take him away. Yes ... yes, I know he fought and struggled, but I wanted to see the bubbles ... just the bubbles, eyes. Then there weren't any more. They were all gone. Please, eyes, now go away ... just leave me alone. Not any more, eyes, not more. Don't bring them back. How they glisten and sparkle, such shiny knives, pretty shiny knives, how sharp, how nice. Ahh, how nice they cut....

Lie still, my pretty. Oh, how nice it was to slice nice even slices from this pretty maid. No, don't scream. Oh, how wonderfully they slice ... each slice so nice and even, just like nice slices of bread. How pretty her blood is ... screams such wonderful streams, and now they are gone, too. Just a few more slices to make.

Oh, eyes, take her away! Please, take her away! The eyes ... I must see the glass. Three minutes ... three minutes ... three minutes.... Now I can get rid of the eyes ... the glass ... the antidote ... the antidote ... life.... I can come back to life ... give me life ... the antidote....

No, no... Please, eyes, not forever....

This first "Shock Tale" must have really shocked, unsettled or, at least, surprised viewers expecting Marvin's monologue to segue into his usual brand of dark comedy. Many of them were glad when the story was over, the tension ended and they could once more relax.

Marvin wasn't the only *Shocktail Party* character to do dramatic readings. On at least one occasion the show's only other speaking character, Orville, did the honors, doing a dramatic reading of Edgar Allan Poe's classic short terror story "The Tell-Tale Heart."

The Ghost, ER, Guest Stars

Shocktail Party had many fans, a lot of them celebrities, some of whom would be performing at the nearby nightclubs Chez Paree on Fairbanks or Mister Kelley's on North Rush Street, or the Chicago Theatre on North State Street, which presented live stage acts in addition to showing first-run movies.

Joy Bennett recalled in the Thomas interview:

> We often had performers from the Chez Paree come over between shows and do a skit along with Marvin and Dear; from memory only — Sammy Davis, Jr., Jack LaLanne, George Raft, and others who were, at the time, headliners. It was very impromptu and always fun!

Bruce Newton related his fond memory of the night Sammy Davis, Jr., made his surprise visit to the *Shock Theatre* dungeon. As Newton described the incident in Okuda and Yurkiw's book, Davis agreed to come down to the WBKB studios and appear in one of the program's skits. Newton, before airtime, outlined for the entertainer the plan for the skit. Davis was supposed to walk down the steps where Marvin always made his opening appearance, kick the prop skeleton (rigged to fall apart), and then sit down in the set's phony electric chair. Then Newton, as Shorty the Frankenstein Monster, would emerge from the shadows to confront the entertainer.

Upon seeing Shorty, Davis was supposed to react fearfully, then say "something"; but, this being live TV, he should be careful about *what* he said. When Newton asked what his response would be, Davis replied, "None of your business. I'll come up with something." As further recounted by Newton to Okuda and Yurkiw,

> So we're on the air, and Sammy is standing in the middle of the dungeon set. Normally. I'd come out growling, but I decided to sneak up on him silently. Sammy was a little guy, and I didn't realize he only weighed about 100 pounds. When I grabbed him and picked him up, I accidentally put him right into the overhead lights. After I put him down, he looked up at me and said, "Man, you're gonna turn me white!" I started laughing uncontrollably.

Newton recalled that he could hear the panic going on behind the relatively thin glass wall of the director's booth, with the director yelling. "Cut to black.... I mean, cut to white ... I mean ... *whatever!*"

Newton told interviewer Rick Thomas that Boris Karloff and Bela Lugosi were among the surprise guests who showed up on *Shock Theatre*. Karloff,

(ş̧C)

however, never appeared on the program, at least no in the flesh. As for Lugosi, Newton remembered him as being kind of "weird." Indeed, poor Bela must have been weird. Because the appearance so vividly recalled by Newton would have been a major feat even for Lugosi, considering the fact that the actor passed away in 1956, more than a year before the first *Shock Theatre* aired.

A Guest from the "Morgue"

One of the most memorable guest appearances, at least for watchers of Chicago local television, occurred on the night of February 7, 1959, the same night that *Shock Theatre* premiered *House of Dracula* (1945), Universal's swan song entry in their series of movies featuring three of their best known horror characters:

> "Tonight's story is called *House of Dracula*," Marvin says, "which just goes to show you that Dracula wasn't all bad. He was family man enough to build his own house. It stars ... Dracula, the Hunchback, Frankenstein's Monster, the Wolf Man ... and Margaret O'Brien."

The surprise guest was local TV celebrity Marty Faye. Faye, often sarcastic, even acerbic, was currently doing his own WBKB variety show on Sunday nights, *Marty's Morgue.*

Like other visitors to *Shock Theatre*, Faye, following the sound of a doorbell ringing, made his grand appearance walking down the cellar stairs. Once nestled amid the dungeon furnishings and props and noting the place's strange occupants, Faye started making comments that were in keeping with his TV image.

> Looking around at Dear and the other denizens of Marvin's cellar, Faye smirks and comments, "So this is what my audience looks like."
>
> Faye tells Marvin that he wants to hire a band for his own show and asks for a recommendation. Marvin suggests the Deadbeats and instructs the band to warm up. Strangely, Faye likes the forthcoming discordant sounds
>
> "It'll sell a million," Faye says. "I can see the gold record now."
>
> "Sorry," responds Marvin, "our colors are black."
>
> When Marvin asks Faye for a contract for the band, Faye replies, "Are you kidding? I've got my own contract troubles."
>
> "How much will they be paid?
>
> Faye quietly discusses money with Orville, then answers, "All the kosher salamis they can eat."
>
> After some more kidding, Faye again checks out his surroundings, makes a face and blurts out, "What a crummy place!"
>
> Marvin, taken by surprise and hardly pleased with Faye's comment, orders Shorty to "Take care of this guy!"

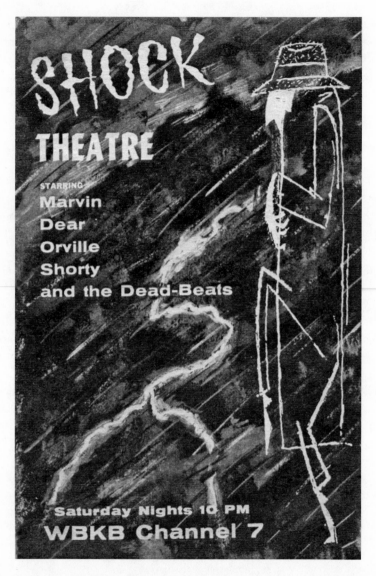

The last full-page advertisement for *Shock Theatre* to appear in *TV Guide* magazine.

Always obedient, Shorty grabs Faye and shoves him into a standing open coffin, at which point Marvin shuts the lid and seals his visitor inside.

Faye, of course, really wasn't looking for a band. The Deadbeats, *sans* their *Shocktail Party* fright makeups, did, in fact, comprise the combo that was providing music for Faye's own show.

11

Continuing Shock Therapy

By 1959, with both *Shock Theatre* and *Shocktail Party* occupying so much of his time, Terry Bennett had settled into his Marvin role and was quite comfortable playing it. As quoted by an uncreated interviewer in the *Chicago Sun-Times*, Terry said with tongue in cheek:

"[Marvin] is a nice fellow, but he's all mixed up, not really evil, but just thinking everyone enjoys hurting people. Doesn't everyone get a boot out of hacking off somebody's fingers?"

... Marvin has startled State Street pedestrians by arriving at the studio in a hearse and being taken out of his coffin on the sidewalk. He also has tied Dear to the miniature railroad tracks in Lincoln Park Zoo, and he intends in the near future to throw her from the roller coaster ride in Riverview Amusement Park.

"That ought to be a barrel of fun," he said.

Another Saturday Night....

A typical *Shock Theatre* program aired on May 2, 1959. Following the first movie break, we returned to Marvin, who was about to take photos of Dear, Orville and Shorty.

Marvin pauses, noting that Dear, although wearing a mask, looks much too pale. Dear, in her unique way of vocalizing, communicates that she is afraid to go out into the daylight.

Marvin has the solution to her problem, a wonderful new sun lamp. He sets Dear under the lamp and explains the importance of using the device sparingly. Leaving the lamp switched on, Marvin walks over to Shorty and Orville to show them his camera.

Meanwhile, the sun lamp begins to overheat. Marvin ignores the crackling sounds. By the time he finally reacts to the sounds, all that is left of Dear is a plate-full of ashes.

135

"How do you like that?" Marvin says. "How is she going to get suntanned if she insists on running out for cigarettes all the time?"

Another skit airing that same night had Marvin reading a book with the title *How to Cure Absent-Mindedness*:

> Setting aside the book, Marvin is about to whip Shorty, when Orville and Dear remind him that he has forgotten his whip.
>
> Marvin picks up a gun and is about to shoot Orville and Dear, when they remind him that he has forgotten the bullets.
>
> A distraught Marvin walks off, pondering his absent-mindedness....
>
> Meanwhile Dear, Shorty and Orville all conspire to turn the tables on Marvin and do away with him. When Marvin returns to the group, they shoot, but he doesn't fall.
>
> Looking towards the audience, Marvin confesses to his viewers, "How do you like that? I'm so absent-minded ... I forgot to bleed."

Yet another skit performed on that same show had the gang crowded around a desk....

> Marvin and the gang are busy doing paperwork. Suddenly the lights go out.
>
> Marvin goes to the fuse box. Although he thinks he has found the correct fuse, Shorty and Orville try to convince him otherwise. To prove himself correct, Marvin has Dear insert her finger in the box. As electricity courses through her body, the lights come back on.
>
> The group return to their desk and resume work.

The *Shocktail Party* portion of the show opened with Marvin finally being on the receiving end of an act of mayhem:

> Dear steps into view and hits Marvin over his head with a club, after which he replies, "This time it's for the Emmys."
>
> A brief sight gag interrupts the goings-on, showing two feet, with Marvin quipping, "Look, Ma, no hands!"
>
> A filmed segment follows, possibly a remote-camera bit or another "Happy Harry" commercial spoof.
>
> The Deadbeats play "Baubles, Bangles and Bows," a spoof, with Terry's new lyrics, of Robert Wright and George Forrest's popular song first heard in the musical *Kismet*, but now having to do with a bow and arrows.
>
> After the song, Marvin and the gang ad-lib their way through the show's first live bit....

Saturday Nights Improv

What's interesting about these 1959 shows is that, except for the carefully scribed "Shock Tales," Terry was by now just writing synopses rather than anything resembling a traditional script, even for the comedy skits involving

Marvin conducts his Deadbeats in a *Shock Theatre Shocktail Party* segment. From left to right, Russell Crandall (harp), Harold Siegel (string bass), Lenny Druss (flute), leader Sam Porfirio (accordion), Patrick Ferreri (guitar) and Clay Campbell (drums). Frank Oakley designed the prop tombstones.

the entire cast. They were just very brief descriptions of what the action would be, sometimes including an important line or two. Terry, Joy, Bruce and Ronny were so "at home" in their strange characterizations that no actual scripting was required. They simply knew what to do and, after getting a sense of the action and the sort of things they were expected to do, did just that, reacting to and playing off one another. In other words, the program was now featuring a series of improvisational exercises. As Bruce Newton told Rick Thomas in his *Filmfax* interview, "We would have a meeting in the middle of the week and would talk over the general theme. We didn't have a script. Only notes, kind of haphazard. We would do an outline."

—✿—

The comedy skit was not really script-written, but was just briefly described by Terry, as in this example from the same *Shock Theater* telecast:

> They decide to play billiards.... Marv and Dear notice that Shorty has a bald spot ... they decide to experiment to grow hair. They mix some bottles ... and grow hair on a billiard ball....

... Decide to work on Shorty ... mix things in his hair ... finally lift up head ... there is no body underneath. Marv gets "cue" stick ... plays billiards with Shorty's head....

Following that segment, and after a commercial, Marvin performed a "Shock Tale," this one inspired by Edgar Allan Poe's "The Pit and the Pendulum":

I can remember as it were yesterday ... or today. I am traveling through an old forest, a forest that lies in the valley. It is getting dark ... it's near dusk. I hear the twitter of birds in the heavy rustling foliage overhead. The soft breeze plays a tune as it sighs among the branches.

I have walked all day. I am tired. Suddenly I come upon a strange house ... black with age, and covered with dead and dying growth. Not a sound is heard, as I step on the unused stone path which leads to the massive front door.

There are no lights to be seen anywhere. And my heart beats faster ... faster ... a steady tattoo on my breast. I look for ... and find the door knocker. I rap three times and I hear the echo ... just as if I'm in a hollow tomb. I push the heavy

Another look at Marvin's Deadbeats: Patrick Ferreri (guitar), Lenny Druss (flute), leader Sam Porfirio (accordion), Russell Crandall (harp), Clay Campbell (drums) and Harold Siegel (string bass).

door ... gently ... gently ... and it quietly opens. There is no protest from its hinges.

I am inside ... and blackness presses against me like converging walls. The entire place is filled with a silent kind of noise. The noise which may come from an inferno of Dante. The soft swishing of material as it moves from place to place ... shuffling feet movement which never becomes the sound of steps. I heard the faint whisper and groan from the blackness ... making my heart beat faster and louder. My breath is labored. I breathe heavily. It's so hard to breathe. Suddenly ... like a great pandemonium ... the moaning ... the screeching ... the rushing of unknown things descended upon me ... and a great and weighted robe is cast over me ... and I fall to the floor. Blackness ... blackness ... I am lost in blackness....

I awake slowly. And I see that I am chained ... heavy chains ... to the floor. I wrench ... I stretch.... The heavy links that bind my ankles rattle, but I am still chained.

My eyes peer. They focus. I look around and find that I am in a small steel-like cubicle. No door... I see small openings on every side. There are eyes ... the glint of eyes watching my every move. And then ... I see what is above me. A pendulum ... swinging ... swinging ... and it's closer ... back and forth.... Each swing brings it closer ... steel ... razor-sharp steel. And it'll cut my body in half ... in two ... with less effort than a sharp knife in a steak....

I cringe for the floor ... and the blade comes closer and closer...

I shiver ... and cold sweat runs down my face. I want to cry ... my body shivers, almost as if I can feel the breath of the blade's edge as it passes my body.

I move. I strain. But the blade is aiming for my body. I cannot evade its swing. The blade is now almost upon me. One swing ... two swings ... and its giant edge will cut me in two. [Perhaps taking a cue from Dear, Marvin screams, as the scene fades to black.] And now, I know the feeling of death."

Following the show's final commercial, Marvin returned to his usual, gleefully maniacal self. Standing by a large wheel of chance, the kind seen on TV quiz programs and at carnivals, Marvin stated that it was time to play "Your Number Is Up!"

> The game, Marvin explains, is a simple one, allowing the contestant to choose the manner in which he or she would like to die. The wheel offers a variety of choices: CHOKE ... ROPE ... GUN ... KNIFE ... POISON ... BOMB.
> Marvin spins the wheel, which finally stops on KNIFE.
> As Marvin congratulates himself on his win, an obliging Shorty quietly sneaks up behind him and rams a knife blade into his back.

A Dungeon Coffeehouse

The *Shocktail Party* had the atmosphere of a beatnik coffeehouse ... of sorts.

Marvin's cellar dungeon was populated by a variety of oddball characters, nonconformists all, some of them clad in black. There was also the music. The Deadbeats' favorite was jazz; and as jazz men, they best excelled, each member of the combo capable of holding his own against any musician in any smoke-filled nightclub or beatnik den in the Windy City.

The coffeehouse environment gave the Deadbeats the perfect venue for ad-libbing through several minutes of pure jazz, accompanied by the gang snapping their fingers and clapping their hands to the beat. Marvin, keeping with his beatnik image, recited some morbidly beat poetry (written, of course, by Terry Bennett). One of these recitations was entitled "How Would You Feel If You Were Dead?"

How would you feel one summer day if you jumped out of bed
And winked to blink, and tried to think, then realized you were dead!
You start to get the headache back, you can hardly breathe a breath.
A heart don't tick, it makes you sick. What is this thing called death?
How would you feel if you were dead, a moment that relaxes?
No breath of air, 'cause it's not there, you don't pay income taxes.

How would you feel if you were dead? You've given up your life.
No garden rake, no teeth to ache, just think, no nagging wife.
It's nice to know that you are dead. The beginning of the end.
There is no strife in daily life, in fact it's the latest trend.
Being dead is lots of fun, or did you ever wonder?

No doctor bills or gaudy frills, you're hidden six feet under.
Being dead is nice to be, you get those dividends.
No aching teeth, a brand new wreath, with lots of worms for friends.
Being dead is loads of fun, your friends will join the game.
So join them all, have a ball, have a gravestone with your name.
You might as well all have some fun, you'll find that time will fly.
Those silly quirks, so shoot the works, don't live it up, just die!

12

Shock Absorbers

Marvin often referred to *Shock Theatre* as "good old Shockaroo Theatre" and to the movies he showed as either "comedies" or "cartoons." Likewise and not surprisingly, he would invent a name for fans of *Shock Theatre*.

It has been stated in print at various times that *Shock Theatre* and its stars had a million or more faithful fans. While that number may have been somewhat of an exaggeration, the show did have an enormous fan following. Just how many *Shock Theatre* fans were "out there," loyally tuning in on Saturday nights, can never be accurately determined. But there were a lot of them. And Marvin dubbed these fans "Shock Absorbers."

Some "Shock Absorbers," more creative than others, began sending in jokes that, oftentimes, Marvin would read on the program. One such joke, written in the style of the era's popular "shut up" jokes, was read by Marvin the night he showed *The Raven* (a Universal Pictures movie of 1935 suggested by Edgar Allan Poe's poem and some of his short stories). It was sent in by fan Bill Hamilton of Chicago suburb Glen Ellyn.

> Marvin is sitting at his desk with his mail, trying to open a letter. Failing in his attempts, he goes over to Dear who, fortunately for him, has a knife sticking in her back.
> He removes the knife and uses it as a letter opener, then reads Hamilton's joke.
> "Dad, what's a werewolf?"
> "Keep quiet — and comb your face."

Among *Shock Theatre*'s more enthusiastic, loyal and prolific fan scribes was Bill Feret, a Chicago teenager whose name, mentioned numerous times by Marvin, would almost achieve the status of celebrity among watchers of the show. The ubiquitous Feret, probably the program's Number One "Shock Absorber," sent in many jokes, original poems and his own new lyrics for well-known songs.

Marvin read one of Feret's pieces, a poem entitled "Shocktail Party," right after relating Hamilton's joke. Then, setting the poem aside, he introduced the night's movie:

> "Tonight's story is called *The Raven*, and it is for the bird. It stars Boris and Bela ... and they'll just kill you.
> "Did you ever notice Bela Lugosi's eyes when he stares at you? Sometimes they look just like lights peering at you..."
> The scene dissolves to the opening of *The Raven*, with an automobile's headlights shining through the darkness of night....

One of Feret's earliest submissions was his rewrite of Clement Clarke Moore's famous poem "The Night Before Christmas" (also known as "'Twas the Night Before Christmas" and "A Visit from St. Nicholas"), first published in 1823. Marvin read Feret's parody, "sent in by a fellow fiend, er, friend," on January 25, 1958, following the conclusion of that night's movie *The Spider Woman Strikes Back*:

> 'Twas the night after *Shock*, and all through the crypt
> No one had started to have the mummies shipped.
> The bodies were hung by the gallows with care,
> In hopes that [*à la* Lugosi] Count Dracula would soon be there
> The zombies were nestled all snug in their tombs
> While visions of vampires flew all 'round the room.
> The moon up on high made the werewolves growl,
> And you could even hear the Night Monster howl.
> And what through my one bulging eye should I see,
> But Count Dracula flying as fast as could be.
> His eyes, how they twinkled, his fangs were so scary,
> His teeth were like diamonds, his face was so hairy ... etc.

Feret eventually got to know Terry and Joy Bennett personally.

The Official Terry Bennett Fan Club

In 1959 Bill Feret launched the "Only Official Terry Bennett Fan Club." In addition to getting an identification card bearing a photograph of Terry as Marvin and his autograph, members also received the first issue of the club journal. Written and edited by the club's president Feret, this "fanzine" was a simple, unpretentious mimeographed affair run off on cheap paper (one side only) that, through time, would yellow and begin to crumble away.

More durable was the small photograph of Marvin that Feret stuck on every front cover. A few more photos were stuck on some of the inside pages.

This is to certify that

[signature]

is a member in good
standing of the

TERRY "MARVIN" BENNETT FAN CLUB

[signature] "Marv" Bennett
President

Identification card — signed circa 2002 — for "The Only Official Terry Bennett Fan Club," started by fan (foremost "Shock Absorber and future professional writer) Bill Feret.

The journal covered much territory in its 15 pages, including a short history of *Shock Theatre* and *The Jobblewocky Place*, biographies of Terry and Joy, drawings of the club mascot (and *Shock* "character," although now on the printed page also possessing a skeletal body) "Mr. Bones," reviews by "Dr. Acula" of current movies, magazine, book and record reviews, shrunken head cartoons, suggestions on how to write newspaper and magazine letters-to-the-editor about the show, several contests, notices about other fan clubs (the Deadbeats and "Horror Heroine" actress Beverly Garland), plus other related items..

Some of Feret's Marvin-inspired "Jokes in a Jugular Vein" were included in the journal:

"And how much would you like to contribute to the Indian Relief Fund, Mrs. Custer?"
"Did you get the license number of that woman who hit you?"
"No, but I'd recognize her laugh anywhere."
"Honey, I hate my sister's guts."
"Shut up, and eat what I give you."

Feret also offered a "Poetry Coroner," featuring the same kinds of verses that he'd been sending into *Shock Theatre* for the past two years:

Mary Had a Little Ghoul

Mary had a little ghoul,
It's [*sic*] skin was smooth as Yul's,
To everything that Mary did
The lamb was sure to drool.
He followed her to the tomb one day,
Which was against the laws,
And you could hear her screaming,
With her inside his jaws.

Gory Laurie

Gory Laurie,
Screaming and cry,
Kissed the ghouls
And made them die.
When the ghouls came back for more
Gory Laurie locked the door.

In a section called "Terry Tells," the fanzine provided information about Terry Bennett, including his date and place of birth, height (five feet, eight and one-half inches [although in reality he was only five feet seven]), weight (152 pounds), and hair and eye color (brown and hazel, respectively). There were even an interview with the man:

Q: Do You Have Any Pets?
A: Yes, I have a cat and a cocker spaniel.

How much time, help, support, etc. do you think an actor owes his fans?
At least 98 percent or more.

How did you get your start in show business?
Mainly through amateur shows.

What is your idea of spending a perfect day?
Relaxing at home, reading, drawing, and mowing or watering the lawn.

How much mail do you receive a day?
Between 5 to 100 letters, and sometimes even more.

If you could have three wishes come true, what would they be?
1. That science would find a cure for Cancer,
2. That people everywhere would find happiness,
3. And perhaps a little selfishly, that I'd have security in life.

What are the names of the Deadbeats, and the instruments that they play?
Sam Porfirio — Accordion; Pat Ferrari [*sic*] — Guitar; Russ Crandall — Harp; Harold Siegal [*sic*] — Bass; Clay Campbell — Drums; and Lenny Druss — Clarinet, Saxophone [*sic*]. And Flute.

Do you have any faults that you find discouraging?
Yes, I'm quick-tempered, and when I want something done, I want it done right away.

How did you go to think of the character "Marvin"?

I thought of a person that the audience would find cynical, yet enjoy. There was no special reason for that particular name, except that I thought the audience would easily remember it.

Is there any truth to the rumor that *Shock* will go off the air?

No, even if we should run out of movies, we'd continue with the Marvin segment alone.

What cities are able to receive *Shock* on their sets?

Illinois, Michigan, Wisconsin, Indiana, and once by a freak of the airwaves, Oklahoma received the show. We even got letters asking to repeat it.

Are you content doing, [*sic*] what you're doing for a living now?

Yes, I'm very, *very* happy.

What are your favorite food [*sic*]? Joy's?

I like beef hot dogs and shrimps, and Joy likes ghoulash [*sic*] and stews.

What's your honest feeling toward "Marvin"?

I'm grateful toward him, and for all he's done for me.

Why has Orville left *Shock*?

There were union troubles or something. I'll try to get him back, but it's doubtful.

A lot of information was packed between the publication's covers. Alas, there were no more issues, and soon, despite the prediction Terry had made in his interview about continuing the Marvin segments, there would soon be no more episodes of *Shock Theatre*.

Loyal Fans

While the show thrived, some of its more ambitious and creative followers devised various, even sneaky ways to "crash" the set and meet Marvin and company. A contemporary newspaper article told of one such fan who, like the Frankenstein Monster, Count Dracula and other characters in the *Shock Theatre* movies, continued to come back: "Currently one young lady hangs around the station three or four times a week in hopes of talking with Terry Bennett. The host of *Shock Theater* and *Jobblewocky Place* is getting weary of sneaking out the back door."

—⚊∿⚊—

Having better luck with her own attempts at meeting Marvin was teenage fan Margaret (Maggie) Walters. Walters would not only meet the cast and crew, she would become a personal friend of Terry and Joy and get to know Bruce Newton, Ronny Born and all of the Deadbeats.

In May of 2006, Walters recalled in an email to the author how she managed to become somewhat of a "fixture" at *Shock Theatre*:

[My friend] had a dysfunctional mother, and her father tried to keep her happy by letting her have a lot of sleepovers with friends, so I spent most of my weekends there with her, watching *Shock Theater*, and eating pizza. It didn't take either of us too long to get so fanatical about *Shock Theater* that we had to meet Marvin. So with the focus typical of adolescent girls, we hauled our asses down to State and Lake Streets, to the WBKB studios.... Where of course we weren't permitted to even get on the elevator.

An enterprising, resourceful and quite determined young lady, Maggie was not about to give up so quickly. Besides, she and her friend were already downtown and the day was far from over.

It was early winter, and very cold, so we went into that drugstore that was on the southwest corner in the ABC building, and were drinking cherry Cokes when the nice policeman came in from the outside. He was funny. He could make his hat move up and down on his head without moving his face. We got to talking to him, and asking him if he could get us upstairs, which of course he said no to. But we kept going down there on Saturdays, and kept nagging him. His name was Tony Guerrero, Anyway, he finally gave in, and said that he'd introduce us to one of the receptionists [and ask] if we could come down on a weekday.

[It was] probably around the Christmas holiday, and we showed up, and Tony took us up and introduced us to Marge [the receptionist], and told her that we desperately needed to meet Marvin. She was not exactly unsympathetic, but gave us a professional run-around. Which didn't stop us, of course.

The "Marge" that Walters and her friend met was probably Marjorie Harris, a WBKB secretary who handled many of the secretarial chores that involved *Shock Theatre*. Eventually Marge gave in to the girls' persistence.

We kept going back there, and it wasn't long before she finally let us talk to either Dick Locke or Richie Victor — both of them directors on the show. Both of whom took pity on us and let us meet Marvin. Since we were both housebroken, and not inclined to making much of a disturbance, they let us back pretty much whenever we wanted after that. Which we did a lot more than we could get away from our assorted parents.

Through Terry, Maggie met Bill Feret, who soon made her secretary of the "Only Official Terry Bennett Fan Club."

Shock Hops

Some "Shock Absorbers" even began dressing up like Marvin and imitating the character. One such *Shock Theatre* fan was John Spelman, a campaign manager for the Elmhurst Youth Center in Elmhurst, a Chicago suburb.

To celebrate its 1958 elections, the Center held a victory dance — a "sock hop" (or as Marvin called such events, a "Shock Hop") wherein attendees customarily removed their shoes. The dance was scheduled for the evening of Saturday, April 12 (the same night that the real Marvin would premiere the movie *Son of Frankenstein*. Spelman showed up at the event dressed like the *Shock Theatre* host.

A contemporary newspaper article, with the heading "Marvin Shocks Youth Center Slate Right Into Office," reported on the affair:

> "Marvin" and his "ghoulfriend," along with other shock candidates, presented a short skit a la *Shock theater* [*sic*] for couples at the sock hop.
>
> Whoopin' 'n hollerin', the Rebel party, led by campaign manager Dick Lewis, you-alled their way through some mighty fast-talking campaign speeches, but the Shocked voters bought Shock party all the way.

The same night, while attendees of the Elmhurst Youth Center event were enjoying themselves on the dance floor, Marvin was walking down the dungeon steps, returning from a different kind of party.

> Marvin has a noose tied around his neck.
>
> "Hello, I'm Marvin," he says. "What a necking party that was. What a joker that skeleton was. Why, if I get my hands on him, I'll feed him ... oh, well, who likes bones anyway?"
>
> He looks around, seeing that, save for himself, the place is empty. "Wonder where she is? Hello, Dear ... did you miss me?"
>
> Dear's hand appears (from behind the camera), holding a gun.
>
> "Oh, there you are. What's that you have in your hand? Did you miss me?"
>
> She fires and, just in time, Marvin ducks.
>
> "Yep, she missed me," he says. "I can't understand it. If she keeps doing things like that, how will we ever see a commercial?"
>
> Marvin does show the commercial, and after it ends....
>
> "Tonight's story is called Son of Frankenstein," he says. "You remember the original Frankenstein. This is the *Son of Frankenstein*. In the weeks to come, we'll meet the grandfather of Frankenstein, the great-grandfather of Frankenstein and, for a grand finale, we'll meet the college chum of Frankenstein.
>
> "I'd like to announce that the characters in tonight's story are fictitious, and as you know, 'fictitious' is just a fancy word meaning lousy. If there's any resemblance to anyone living or dead ... they're better off dead. But first I must tell you a bedtime story. This is the story of Hansel and Gretel ... and they lived in a quaint little house on the outskirts of the cemetery...."

Marvin, or at least young men impersonating the character, were materializing all over Chicago and outlying areas, showing up at parties, dances and other social gatherings. It was time for the *real* Marvin to get out of his own "quaint little house"— at least, that is, out of his dungeon.

Guest-Starring Marvin

Terry Bennett began showing up on radio disc jockey programs where, as Marvin, he responded to fans calling in to make comments and ask questions. Also, Terry made appearances on local television shows other than *Shock Theatre*. Community Discount Department Stores, a local Chicago retail chain, were known for low prices and much less than top-of-the-line merchandise. At one time before becoming Marvin, Terry had worked for Community, handling the chain's promotions.

Community was also the sponsor of *Outer Space Theater*, a WBKB daytime television show. Each Sunday the show ran a chapter of one of Universal's three Flash Gordon theatrical serials starring Larry "Buster" Crabbe: *Flash*

Marvin (Terry Bennett) makes an appearance on local Chicago radio station WAIT ("820 on your dial").

Gordon (1936), *Flash Gordon's Trip to Mars* (1938) and *Flash Gordon Conquers the Universe* (1940). During their show's run, Community even arranged for Crabbe to appear and sign autographs at some of their store locations.

The show was hosted by Larry Goodman, who founded the chain in 1946. In addition to running the Flash Gordon episodes, the program featured an "outer space quiz": Goodman, on camera and over the telephone, quizzed viewers who tried giving the correct answers and win various prizes.

One Sunday, "Shock Absorbers," who happened to be tuning in to watch their space hero Flash Gordon, had an unexpected treat. Community was promoting a big sale the stores were having on April 1. The Flash Gordon installment ended with, as always, Flash and/or his friends in some perilous predicament. Now it was time for the "outer space quiz."

On this day, however, something was different.

Instead of the television image cutting to the owner of Community sitting at his telephone, the scene was of lightning crashing ... followed by a shot of an old haunted house ... all backed by screams, rattling chains and familiar music. Then the scene cut to inside the house ... and a familiar dungeon with a familiar flight of stairs.

And coming down the stairs was Marvin!

Had something gone haywire at WBKB? Had *Shock Theatre* been rescheduled, moved from its nighttime Saturday timeslot to the brightness of a Sunday afternoon? Had someone at the station thrown the wrong switch or pushed the wrong button and replaced *Outer Space Theater* with that other *Theatre*?

There was a much simpler explanation, which became clear when Marvin sat down at a table and started working the telephone. Because of the upcoming April Fool's Day, Marvin would be hosting the "outer space quiz "

Like Flash's rocket ship, ratings for *Outer Space Theater* must have soared that Sunday afternoon.

Marvin and Dear—Live and in Person!

Terry and Joy Bennett started going out — that is, outside of their studios at WBKB.

The husband-and-wife team made numerous personal appearances, as Marvin and Dear or just as themselves, at a variety of events. They showed up in Chicago's annual State Street Christmas parade, arrived at WBKB in a rented hearse accompanied by a police motorcade and played basketball with the Harlem Globetrotters.

At eight o'clock on the night of Tuesday, August 2, 1958, Terry, through the efforts of dance chairman Douglas Duerr, appeared as himself ("'Marvin'

Minus Specs" as a newspaper item reported the next day) to host the Twin Cities Area Young Republicans' Back to School Hop, one of the group's monthly dances held in St. Joseph, Michigan. Admission was 75¢ per person or $1.25 a couple.

In addition to meeting "Terry Bennett, 'Marvin' of T-V *Shock Theater*," as the fliers boasted, dance attendees also got free refreshments, music by Roger Kunde and Band, and a chance to win a door prize (a "V M HI FI PORTABLE RECORD PLAYER").

On the 23rd of the same month, Terry and Joy, as themselves and with Red Flannels tagging along, appeared in person at two of Chicago's Shoppers World stores to promote the retail chain's "Fall Carnival of Values." Fans could meet the Bennetts and Red and receive "FREE AUTOGRAPHED PHOTOS!" from one to two P.M. at the store's Cermak Road and Austin location and from three to four P.M. at the Milwaukee Avenue at Foster Avenue and Central Street location.

On the weekend of May 22 through 24, 1959, Terry Bennett appeared at the second annual Northwest Home and Garden show, held at the Arlington Park Jockey Club. Also on the bill was Tommy Leonetti, an actor as well as one of the popular singing stars of the television show *Hit Parade*. According to an April 30 newspaper article

> [Bennett] will bring both his happy-go-lucky puppet from *Jobblewocky Place* and the statuesque blonde, Joy, of *Shock Theatre*....
> Joy, who on the show has more lives than a cat, is in reality Mrs. Bennett. The pair lives a happy life, but to a million TV viewers every Saturday night, Joy becomes the object of Marvin's fiendish machinations. Marvin has been portrayed by *Time*, *The Saturday Evening Post* and *Life* as one of the foremost monsters on TV. *Shock Theatre* has consistently rated at the head of the top 10 programs on Chicago TV.

Presentations witnessed by the Bennetts at this event included a fashion show, a competition of garden clubs and a helicopter demonstration. Afterwards they returned to downtown Chicago in time to host the *Son of Shock!* movie scheduled for that night—*Black Friday*, a story about human brain transplantation mixed with familiar gangster shenanigans. It starred *Shock Theatre's* two biggest superstars, Boris Karloff and Bela Lugosi.

At times, when they weren't working at the station or doing personal appearances, Terry and Joy got to enjoy a vacation. Yet even when they did manage to get away from their WBKB workload and slip off on their own, their celebrity status often preceded them.

Dan Golden, now a prolific motion picture producer, writer and director living in California, watched *Shock Theatre* as a child from his family's home in Carpentersville, Illinois. He recalled for the author:

[Terry Bennett] stayed at my grandmother's cottage in Wisconsin once. I didn't actually meet the guy, but the next time my brother and I stayed with her, we'd say things to each other like, "That's the bed Marvin slept on." or, "That's the toilet Marvin sat on."

As *Shock Theatre* continued through 1959, some of the burden on its cast and technical crew was eased as the later programs were videotaped instead of going out live. The show was taped during the day during the week. As Terry Tiz told me, "I could go to the Saturday night live broadcast any time my parents would let me, but when they started taping the show, I couldn't go because of school. No more *Shock* shows to go watch ... very sad indeed."

—⚉—

As to whether any videotapes of the show still exist, no one has yet managed to turn one up, even though searches have been made at what is now WLS-TV. Tiz remains pessimistic:

I doubt if ABC has any tapes. Back in those days, money was everything to most TV stations, so they would reuse video tapes over and over. "Archive?? What for?" They would think, or not give it any thought. Typical thinking of the times. Only possibility would be if someone kept a tape for their own personal collection....

I remember one of the [Deadbeats] members saying (and I paraphrase), [ABC has] got this $10,000 camera lens sitting around collecting dust and they won't pay an extra three dollars for the day so a musician can play a banjo part

By the fall of 1959, with *Shock Theatre* still thriving, and Terry and Joy also doing many personal appearances, fans must have taken it for granted that the program — like such immortal fiends as Frankenstein's Monster, Count Dracula and the Mummy — would go on eternally. But, as has often been said, no good things last forever, even a good thing like *Shock Theatre*.

"Shock Absorbers" were about to receive a jolt.

13

Shockingly Sad News

Late 1959 would be a distressing time for fans of *Shock Theatre*.

Although rumors had already hinted that *Shock Theatre* might be dropped, no official WBKB announcements to that effect had been issued.

Terry Bennett, in his interview with Bill Feret, said that he felt that the show was in no danger of cancellation.

Thus, in the summer of 1959, at least in as much as the show's fans were concerned, the future of *Shock Theatre* seemed to be secure.

Taking "Shock Absorbers" by utter surprise, the stunning bombshell exploded on July 24, 1959, in *Chicago Sun-Times* reporter Jerry Atking's article bearing the ominous headline "*Shock Theatre* Strikes Out in Favor of Cuban Baseball":

> Live it up, kids! Get your fill of *Shock Theatre* and its owl-eyed host, Marvin, before October 31. Seems there's a limit to the number of times even Marvin, Orville, Shorty and the Deadbeats can suffer through old horror flicks.
>
> It's being shoved off the air for lack of fresh (?) material. Tomorrow night must be the fourth time around for *The Mummy's Tomb*. Ditto every Frankenstein and Dracula entry.
>
> Before parents start rejoicing, WBKB is throwing in a replacement sure to keep most of the boys still howling for an extra bonus of TV at 10 P.M. every Saturday.
>
> Beginning on that date, Winter Baseball, Cuban game-of-the-week taped at Grand Stadium in Havana, will be re-telecast over WBKB the Saturday following.

How depressingly ironic it was that *Shock Theatre* was to end just two weeks before the night that pint-sized versions of Frankenstein's Monster, Dracula and the Wolf Man, even Marvin himself, would be prowling the streets of Chicago and its suburbs: Halloween.

Even more depressing, *Shock Theatre* would be replaced by Cuban — not even good old *American!*— baseball: Augmenting the injury with yet further insult, this dubious replacement would not even be an original telecast of the sporting event, but, (*gasp!*) a *videotaped rerun!*

As the weekends approached that dreaded final night, *Shock Theatre* fans began to experience more near-traumatic changes.

Exit, Orville and the Deadbeats

By fall of 1959 the Orville character was dropped from the *Shock Theatre* and *Shocktail Party* cast, apparently (as Terry Bennett had already suggested that year in his interview with Bill Feret) over some union-related issue that Ronny Born had been unsuccessfully trying to solve. Perhaps it had something to do with the fact that, unlike Joy Bennett and Bruce Newton, Born had an actual *speaking* role.

Born's departure from the show was soon followed by that of the Deadbeats. Rumors would circulate for decades that the six musicians left because they all hated wearing (and were unrecognizable under) the zombie-like makeup. These rumors do not appear to be grounded in any truth, although at least one member of the combo was certainly not fond of wearing the get-up.

As Terry Tiz remembered, based upon his own personal knowledge of the Deadbeats members:

> Can't speak for all the fellows, but at least one musician hated the costume, makeup, skits. "Good musicians would much rather just play well, and have an audience appreciate it. We don't really like Show Business, costumes, antics, and spectacle. We 'accompany' Show Biz because we have to ... but, given a choice, we would prefer to perform for a discriminating, intently listening audience." But, "we do (at times) get a kick out of it (Show Biz)."
>
> From what I remember *and* what the band members tell me, the working relationship between the band and Marvin was very good. Same can be said with the staff, writers, and all. The boys were there to provide music the audience would appreciate, and do their best.

Other rumors have suggested that there was friction or even animosity between the Deadbeats members and Terry Bennett, resulting in the band leaving the show. These stories also seem unfounded. Maggie Walters recalled from her visits to the *Shock Theatre* set:

> As far as the Deadbeats and Ronny, I think there might have been some problems, but that was very subtle, and *never* spoken about. The last few months of *Shock*, it seemed that there was noticeably less camaraderie between the Deadbeats and the rest of them, and I noticed that the Deadbeats were kind of hanging more with themselves rather than integrating with everyone else. Today I

want to say that at the time I had the feeling that it had something to do with money more than personalities. I used to talk to Sam Porfirio more than any of the rest of them. And I have a vague feeling that once or twice he might have mentioned something in that vein to me, but I honestly can't say for sure.

Probably a more practical reason — one based on simple economics — may explain the Deadbeats's departure. Members of the combo, like other employees of WBKB, were expected to work when told to do so and for no additional pay. But Saturday night, when the show aired, was traditionally the best time for professional musicians in terms of paying gigs. By spending their Saturday nights at the station playing without additional compensation, the six musicians were missing out on all the lucrative jobs they would otherwise be picking up in Chicago's night spots. As Terry Tiz explained:

> Before the ABC/WBKB times, and after, they all were working Chicago musicians. The list of accomplishments would be long (studio sessions with Frank Sinatra, TV and radio commercials, side men on various recordings).
> These fellows were very well known in the Chicago music scene. The reason A.F. of M. put a "freeze" on the ABC/WBKB musicians was simple. These were the best of the best union musicians in town, so ABC would use them exclusively, allowing other musicians to take gigs around town. A.F. of M. wanted to spread out the work. Their thinking was, these guys would work during the day and pick up other gigs at night, thus not giving other musicians a chance to work.

Also, situations were changing at WBKB and local television stations in general. According to Tiz:

> [L]ocal live shows were expensive and beginning to die out. So there was less call for staff musicians. At one time ABC had over 100 musicians on staff. At the time of *Shock* there were about 40 on call. So as the local shows requiring music died out, staff musicians were released. Based on what Pat [Ferreri] said, it was a money thing. The times they were a-changin.' Who needed "live" music for local shows? Think of the savings, no union musicians to pay.

Shock Around the Clock

With one character and, more significantly, the music gone, WBKB started playing havoc with *Shock Theatre*, moving the show around various new timeslots (i.e., 11:00, 11:30 and even midnight), sometimes even pre-empting it for sporting events. These time switches constituted just another nail driven in the show's coffin. The later timeslots prevented many younger fans, who were not allowed by their parents to stay up *that* late even on a Saturday night, from seeing the program.

One young "Shock Absorber" complained in the letters section of a local television guide booklet:

> I am only 10 years old. I enjoy television very much. Please get *Shock Theater* back on a [*sic*] earlier time so I can watch it. I like Marvin very much.
>
> Yours truly,
> Gary Lang

Young Gary was but one of many *Shock Theatre* fans now faced with the same problem: They couldn't watch their favorite TV show any more.

By late 1959, the number of viewers watching *Shock Theatre* mattered little or not at all to the station's brass. It was in its final lap and WBKB needed to prepare for its new scheduling line-up.

The Dreaded Swan Song

Shock Theatre did not leave the airwaves in the proverbial blaze of glory, at least when considering the film that was chosen to be shown on the program's final night.

Almost until the very end of its two-year run, the show had provided "Shock Absorbers" with a weekly dose of horror movies from the 1930s and 1940s, most of them made by Universal Pictures or Columbia Pictures. Some of those films — like the original *Frankenstein, Dracula, The Mummy, The Invisible Man* and *Bride of Frankenstein*— were unquestionably classics. The show also, on occasion, ran some very fine horror movies made by other studios, including the classy *Hangover Square* and moody Val Lewton–produced *I Walked With a Zombie* and *The Body Snatcher.*

On that portentous night of October 17, 1959, however, again in its original 10:00 timeslot, *Shock Theatre* presented a film that could hardly be deemed a classic, classy, moody or even mediocre. In fact, it was the absolute worst movie the show had ever run.

The movie for that final night was a re-showing of the notorious Edward D. Wood Jr.'s *Bride of the Monster.* By showing it on *Shock Theatre's* last night, WBKB demonstrated that they no longer cared about the series that had premiered with the Boris Karloff classic *Frankenstein.*

Marvin again introduced himself, the show and the movie; but this time his demeanor sounded a bit more serious than usual:

> H'lo! I'm Marvin. Tonight is a very, very special night. I would just like to tell you that if during the past two years you've wanted to see what Dear looks like, I promise you that tonight is the night. Because tonight ... is our last appearance. Shorty ... Dear ... and mine on good ol' 'Shockaroo Theatre.' Three years

ago we made a promise that on our last appearance we would show what Dear looks like. And so tonight ... we will show her. If you know anyone who wants to see what Dear looks like, call them ... and tell them that tonight ... is the night.

However, if we're really here or not does not really matter. Because on television screens everywhere you'll be seeing this sort of thing. It's really a shock. But I thought, because it's our last appearance here, our last show, even though the cartoons are still being shown, that we ought to have a different kind of show tonight. So in addition to showing Shorty, what he is, showing what he looks like and your face and everything, how can we look different? And we will have something real different tonight. The name of the cartoon is called *Bride of the Monster*. And it starts off like most cartoons do. It starts off with a little rain, a little cloudiness, just like this....

Bride of the Monster started, then ran his creaky course, breaking as all the previous movies had done on *Shock Theatre*, with Marvin and the gang performing their usual kinds of skits. When the movie reached its end, Marvin sat down at the set's table, Dear seated beside him, and directly addressed the program's TV audience.

Shock Theatre, *R.I.P.*

For years Marvin had been teasing his audience, stating that the following week viewers would get to see the true face of the woman he'd always been tormenting. Of course, whenever a past moment for unmasking arrived, some technical mishap would occur (*e.g.,* an out-of-focus camera, a light going out, and so forth). Tonight, however, there were to be no such glitches.

Also, there would be no *Shocktail Party*.

Marvin spoke directly to his viewers at home:

And that was our cartoon for the night. And you know, earlier today we said that, after two years, Shorty and Dear and I are going to be leaving you. And that means you can't be hideous all your life, you know [*laughs*]. So we thought that this was a good time ... to forget about Marvin ... and kill Marvin off....

As those last words were spoken, Marvin's shrill, high-pitched and hyperactive voice changed, metamorphosing back to the lower, calmer and mellower voice children knew from weekday mornings and older audiences had heard back in December of 1957 on that debut show *Shock Theatre*— the voice of just a normal man named Terry Bennett. There was also a genuinely sincere tone to Terry's voice now as he took off his dark glasses and smiled....

And living like normal people means ... thank you, Gingis Brothers, thank-yous are a hard thing to say.... There's so many people you have to thank. At

Shock Theatre we met quite a bunch of people. People who were directly responsible for putting us on the air....

The directors, dear friend Dick Locke, Richie Victor and our good friend who directed tonight's show, Dick Dumont. Thank you very, very much. And sitting next to our director is our technical director Chuck Kaiser on the first shows ... and dear old Cliff Vogel is doing the job right now. Do I look good, Cliff? Jim Daugherty is the man who permits you to hear me and everything else that happens here. Thank you. Jim, our audio man. Thanks to all the stagehands who've worked with us. I think without our stagehands, many of our effects would not have been ... would not have come across. Thank you, stagehands.

And thanks, of course, to all the brass at WBKB. And that's Mr. Veracker, "Red" Quinlan, Dan Schuffman, everyone else responsible.

I would also like to thank.... These are names to you, I know, but they are very important to me. Names like Carl Carlton, my associate writer. Thank you, Carl, for many ideas and gimmicks you've come up with. And all the gunshots and strange sounds you heard belong to the sound effects men like Roger Jensen, none better in the business. And our floor men, too, who have been wild enough trying to count the seconds as they tick by to see that we get on on time and get off on time.

And forgotten people like the Deadbeats, who are no longer with us. And Orville, played by Ronny Born. And Shorty ... big Shorty ... Bruce Newton. Bruce?

At that point Terry and the still-masked Joy looked off camera and heard the familiar growl of the show's resident Frankenstein Monster.

"Shorty" lumbers into the scene continuing to growl, maintaining the character.

"This is Bruce Newton," Terry reveals. "I've been asked so many times how tall you are, Bruce. And I must admit it's four feet six in his stocking feet. But he is wearing a mask."

Terry offers to take off Newton's mask, but "Shorty" would rather do the job himself. He yanks off the rubber Frankenstein Monster mask, only to expose another.

"Bye, Bruce," says Terry as the hulking figure stalks off camera, "Bye, Shorty. One of the nicest people in show business, Bruce Newton. And then there's the young lady ... whom I'm married to, whose face has never been seen. This is Dear. Honey?"

The rest of that final show belonged exclusively to Terry and Joy.

This was the moment that so many *Shock Theatre* aficionados had been waiting for (and at the same time dreading, because of the finality associated with it). They were about to see what Dear looked like, but that revelation would also signal the end of that character as well as that of the show.

At last, "Dear" removed her frilly, silvery mask to unveil the lovely smiling face of Joy Bennett.

"Hi," says Terry.

Joy, still using her Dear "baby talk" voice, replies with something sounding vaguely like, "Hello, Marvin."

Marvin jokes for a few moments with Joy, then says, "The mask is off."

"The mask is off," answers Joy in her real voice.

"The mask is off," Terry repeats.

"I can talk at last."

Laughing, Terry agrees, "That's right."

"You know, I've been talking the other way so long, I was beginning to like it."

"Boy, I was beginning to understand it!"

"Well, doesn't everyone?"

Terry laughs again, then asks, "How does it feel now that the mask is off?"

"At last I can breathe. And besides, I was getting a complex every time I passed a mirror. I was frightened!"

"You must be kiddin.'"

The final moments of *Shock Theatre* were creeping closer, and too rapidly, it seemed.

Terry and Joy continued for a while with their friendly banter, playing nicely off each other's comments, reacting naturally and lovingly and humorously. In some later decade this husband-and-wife team might have been the stars of some network–TV morning talk show. Alas, such programs did not exist back in 1959. (ιυcoRRεcт)

Then, for one last time, the subject of Marvin and Dear arose.

"Now we can go back to living as Mr. and Mrs. Terry Bennett," Terry tells Joy. "No more Marvin."

"You wouldn't rather go back to Marvin and Dear?"

"Listen, Marvin treated his wife terribly. He cut your fingers off, cut your throat...."

And, following some more joking conversation....

"Now we can live like normal people, sit home Friday nights and watch the *Shock* movies on TV. Hmm?"

"Oh, heavens no, I'd never do that!" says Joy.

"Why not?

"I'd be frightened."

Terry chuckles. "Come on, dear, it's getting late."

"Is it over?"

"We'd like to thank you," Terry says to the audience, "so very much ... for making us what we were. These were the happiest two years of our life. Thank you very much. Goodbye."

It was indeed over. With those last words, spoken by Terry Bennett as he and Joy walked off camera, *Shock Theatre* came to its end.

In Name Only

Or *was* it all really over? Terry Bennett had, after all, said on that final show something about the "cartoons" continuing to be shown on *Shock Theatre*. How could that be if the show were really dead?

As "Shock Absorbers" were soon to learn, although Marvin, Dear and Shorty were now past history, a show still bearing the name *Shock Theatre* would turn up on Channel 7 but now moved to 1:00 am on Friday nights. The dungeon sets remained standing and the same old movies continued to be shown. And there was still a host ... or at least a person whom some people might have assumed to be a replacement for Marvin.

The first movie run on the relocated *Shock Theatre* was a familiar one, *The Mummy's Ghost.*

In place of the black-clad guy with the glasses, standing amid the familiar walls of that cellar dungeon, was a normal-appearing man wearing, of all things, a business suit. This new guy on the old set didn't tell macabre jokes or perform acts of mayhem. He was simply a fast-talking local–TV pitchman, a kind of real-life "Happy Harry," whose job was to hawk automobiles for the show's current sponsor, Steve Mitchell Ford.

Like villagers they'd seen in some of the Frankenstein and Mummy movies shown on *Shock Theatre*, fans retaliated, although picking up pens and pencils rather than torches and pitchforks. Soon after the departure of the Bennetts and Bruce Newton, letters began appearing in local newspapers and TV guides. Scribes of all ages were expressing their feelings about the show's cancellation, *almost* all of them fans craving to see more of their *Shock Theatre* heroes:

> We want *Shock Theater* back on the air! I don't understand why it went off. If it's because of winter baseball or football, why couldn't they have it on at another time of day? What happened to Orvil [*sic*] and the Dead Beats [*sic*]? Just before shock [*sic*] went off the air, Orvil [*sic*] wasn't in the show and neither were the Dead Beats [*sic*]. *Shock* isn't very good without them.
>
> S. F. and J.L.

> I used to look forward on Saturday night to seeing a short man in a black turtleneck sweater with thick glasses, a pretty lady with a mask, a very tall man called "Shorty," and a band of men — some with fangs — dressed in black suits. I'm talking about *Shock Theater*. Bring it back!
>
> Joel Bloom

> I enjoyed *Shock Theater* very much. Kindly put in on again. I would be pleased if you did.
>
> Josephine Urban

> Why no action in regard to the return of *Shock?* Man, that was the high spot of Saturday evening, and we must, simply must, have it back.

There are many, many fans hungry for *Shock*— more than you think. Get with
it.

H. Hayes

I used to look forward to Saturday nights, but no more. There's no more
*Shock*s!

A Sad Fan Recently in *TV Week* someone sent his love to *Shock Theater*. The
note was answered, "What is this thing called love?" Well, I'll tell you what it is.
There isn't any better word to express what a wonderful job Marvin, Dear,
Shorty, Orville, and the Dead Beats did on *Shock Theater*. To me it was the best
program on the air. I agree completely with C. S. and express my love and
respect to Terry Bennett, Joy Bennett, Bruce Newton, Ronny Born, and Sam
Porfirio's band.

S. M.

Three cheers for C. S. I want *Shock* back.

Snooker

I don't know who all these birds are who want *Shock Theater* back on the air.
I've never been so happy to see a show go. My husband and I visit with another
couple almost every Saturday and, until *Shock Theater* went off the air, those two
lunkheads [our husbands] never spoke to us, they just sat there watching these
monsters.

Mrs. R. A.

Watched the new *Shock Theater* and predict it'll be off the air in two weeks.
The show needs an M.C. like Marvin to keep it alive.

Marvin was the reason I watched it in the past, and until the men at Channel
7 put an M.C. on the show, I guess I'll put up with the wrestling.

Late Evening Watcher

Even upper-echelon "Shock Absorbers" Bill Feret and Maggie Walters did
their best to bring Marvin and company back:

> [W]e did everything we could do to get them to bring [*Shock Theatre*] back. I
> remember going on the Marty Faye show late one night (kind of the Jay Leno of
> the late '50s–early '60s in Chicago broadcasting), with Bill, trying to enlist sup-
> port from his audience to bring back *Shock*, but that was, as you know, unsuc-
> cessful.

It did not take long for the Steve Mitchell Ford huckster to depart the
old dungeon; and with his leaving, the still-faithful "Shock Absorbers" no
longer saw the show's sets, except in still photos or in their memories.

Shock Theatre, even without any replacement horror host, car salesman
or otherwise, continued to air through the early months of 1960. Still going
by that venerable name, it continued to rerun the old movies from the *Shock!*
and *Son of Shock!* packages, but the showings soon moved still later, to a 1:00
A.M. time slot, sandwiched in between a new variety show starring the ubiquitous Marty Faye and an informational program catering to insomniacs, *A*

Matter of Sleep. Ironically, *Shock Theatre*, at least the show calling itself that, was back on Saturdays — but only in the very early morning.

This version of *Shock Theatre* still opened with the familiar stock shot of lightning and a look at the haunted house, accompanied by the old sound effects and music. Soon the haunted house would go, with just the lightning and sounds of thunder opening the show.

Regardless of the show's title, without Terry and Joy Bennett this was no longer *Shock Theatre*. The very late-night show calling itself *Shock Theatre* soon slipped into obscurity, faded away into final cancellation and was mostly forgotten.

The *Shock!* and *Son of Shock!* movies would remain in WBKB's film library — at least until their licensing period expired and some other local Windy City channel bought them up.

A Shocking Tradition

There were, however, new attempts by other Chicago television stations to recoup some of the glory (and ratings) left behind by *Shock Theatre*. Nevertheless, many fans still longed, although futilely, for a return of their beloved original.

As early as April 15, 1961, less than two years after *Shock Theatre*'s cast of characters departed, the *Chicago Sun Times*' Paul Malloy reported on the situation in his "It's the Malloy" column, that day with the headline "Horror Set to Have a Night of It." As Malloy suggested, new shows were on the way that might placate those old "Shock Absorbers":

> I haven't seen a Nixon-for-President button around town for at least two weeks. Sooner or later the loss of a cause is realized and the crusaders turn to other things.
>
> Not so the adherents of *Shock Theater* in Chicago. At least once monthly I get a long petition for its revival containing so many names I suspect the leaders are cribbing from the Mundelein phone book. Devotees of the Terry Bennett genre don't seem to realize that all the novelty formats must eventually play themselves out. For a while there, *Shock Theater* was threatening to hurl a wave of mummyism across the land.
>
> ... But if it's any consolation to *Shock Theater*ites, Ch. 5 rings up the curtain Saturday night (10:15) on a new horror movie series called *Thrillerama*. The debut will deliver Bela Lugosi, Basil Rathbone and their little playmates in *The Black Sleep*.

Malloy went on to plug such returning shows as *Alfred Hitchcock Presents* and *Twilight Zone* (the latter expanded from 30 minutes to an hour), a new series

of color TV remakes of black and white suspense motion picture classics
including *Spellbound, Notorious, The Spiral Staircase* and *The Paradine Case*,
and the new horror series *Way Out*— admirable shows all. And *The Black Sleep*
(1956) was certainly a fun movie in the "old school" tradition, with a cast also
including Lon Chaney, Jr., John Carradine and that new horror guy from
Bride and the Monster, Tor Johnson.

But none of these shows was *Shock Theatre.*

—ᗰ—

Although *Shock Theatre*— at least with its crazy gang of characters — was
not going to return to Chicago television, many viewers who'd watched the
program still loved the old movies that Marvin ran and retained in their hearts
a spot for the species of master of ceremonies that would, over the years, come
to be known as "horror host."

Why Did They Go?

Why, then, did Terry and Joy Bennett really leave *Shock Theatre?*
Most television shows get cancelled for the same reason — low ratings.
But the numbers for *Shock Theatre* remained relatively high. Also, a show
bearing the name *Shock Theatre*, in the same time slot and using the same
sets and showing the same old movies, continued to air for months on WBKB
following the cast departures.

Terry and Joy leaving *Shock Theatre* apparently was their own decision.
Before they left, their interests seem to have been drifting farther and farther
away from the program.

By 1961 salient changes were occurring in Terry and Joy's personal lives,
changes that also had a bearing on their professional careers. They had already
moved from their Ashland Avenue apartment to a more spacious residence —
a simple five-room house in a Chicago area known as Schiller Park. There,
at night after finishing his official duties every day at WBKB, in a makeshift
office set up in the basement, Terry continued to work out new ideas and
scripts for both *The Jobblewocky Place* and potential new television projects.

Terry and Joy also had a new kind of audience, indeed an audience that
was even younger than the one that faithfully watched *The Jobblewocky Place*
every weekday morning. In October of 1960, following a nine-month wait
following their application, the Bennetts adopted a baby son named Kip.

At first the Bennetts' new addition seemed unappreciative of Terry's ability to entertain. As reported in "A 'Deadbeat' Makes Good with a Dummy,"

Terry and Joy Bennett, about a year after *Shock Theatre* ended, exiting the WBKB-TV building located at 190 North State Street in downtown Chicago.

a feature article published in the May 6, 1961, *Chicago Life* (the weekend supplement magazine of the *Chicago Daily News*):

> The first few days Kip spent with his new family, Terry did every facial imitation he knew without any response from his new son. Terry panicked at the thought that his son was sneering at his acting talent, until his wife told him babies can't see when they are only 5 days old.

Terry and Joy had been advised by some of their friends against bringing a baby into their lives, predicting that they would be "giving up so much" as parents. The Bennetts found that warning to be silly, Kip actually adding much to their lives. Of course the addition of a third family member required some adjustments. For example, Joy reduced her *Jobblewocky Place* appearances from five days per week to three, spending the remaining days at home with to Kip.

As far as Marvin was concerned, Terry, now a happy father, had somewhat different opinions and feelings about the character he had created and developed, and was also concerned over repercussions he had experienced while playing that role. As he explained in that same *Chicago Life* feature story:

> Though the audience reaction to Marvin, Dear ... and the Deadbeats was strong (the Marvin Fan Club drew up a petition with thousands of signatures and took it to the head of the station to beg for the reinstatement of *Shock Theater*) Terry found Marvin a difficult role to play. He says it took three days to just get into the mood to play the role. Terry received phone calls at 4 A.M. from Marvin fans, mostly teenagers, and finally had to resort to an unlisted phone. Ghoulish letters and presents poured in. "It almost changed the kind of person I am," claims Terry. "I'm a ventriloquist who likes to entertain kids, and playing Marvin at night didn't impress parents about my morning show for their children. They thought I really was crazy like Marvin," he says.

Joy Bennett offered her own explanation to Rick Thomas:

> Although the show had great notoriety, it was not a show that we would have wanted to do forever. Terry would not have wanted to be typecast as just a horror show host. He was — first, last and always — a ventriloquist and actor. When we moved to New York, he was able to get involved in producing, directing, and inventing those ideas that lent themselves so well to the TV audience.

The answer to why the Marvin character vacated *Shock Theatre* may be more complex. As Maggie Walters told the author, based upon her own personal relationship with the Bennetts.

> Terry was a highly intelligent, extremely talented, sensitive man.... A lot of highs, usually when he was on camera, and serious lows in between.... I think part of his depression was fed by the fact that he never attained the kind of success in his media that his talent deserved, too, and that must have been very frustrating for him.... He was immensely attractive, charming, talented, intelligent, and all those appealing things. Perhaps even more appealing because of his sensitivity and vulnerability.

"Red" Letter Day

It must have been frustrating for someone with Terry Bennett's abilities, good looks and personal appeal to spend his first two years basically behind the camera relegated to such duties as designing logos and promoting network variety shows and TV Westerns. The man was also having to kowtow to WBKB policy. Terry was a staff employee and had to follow the often dictatorial orders of the station's bosses.

Although Kerry Bennett recalled his mother Joy only speaking highly of WBKB general manager Sterling "Red" Quinlan, a letter written by Quinlan may exemplify the kinds of demands that executive made upon his employees. Dated September 26, 1962, almost three years after the Bennetts left *Shock Theatre*, it was sent not only to Terry, but also to numerous other WBKB staffers, some of them very popular local celebrities. Other recipients of Quinlan's missive included Jim and Bud Stewart, Hal and Nancy Berg, Alex Dreier, Jim Conway, Norman Ross, Joe Slattery, Marty Faye, Betty Caywood, Lynn Walker, Warren Culbertson, Cordon Parenwall, Bob Lendowski, Stuart Brent and even the nationally well-known columnist Irv Kupcinet:

> Gentle people:
> Don't know what you'll be doing December 21 or 23, but I know what you'll be doing on Saturday, December 22....
> You will be appearing at the United Cerebral Palsy Christmas party at the Prudential assembly hall.
> You will be doing it because you're nice people and because you know that I am Executive Vice President of UCP under Arthur Rubloff and because you wouldn't want to let down two nice guys like Rubloff and Quinlan.
> From Rubloff some day you may want real estate. From Quinlan you may want to keep your job; or a good recommendation if you get fired from this one....
> So, stand by, gentle people, and lend a hand to a good cause. I'll give you specific details soon. Party is during the day.
>
> Red Quinlan

Quinlan's letter, unless written in jest (which is doubtful), must have been poorly received by at least *some* of the WBKB employees, and must also have been another blow to Terry's self-esteem. Perhaps there was at least a modicum of consolation for Terry knowing that, as a recipient of his boss' letter, he was numbered among such highly regarded company.

Another blow came to Terry less than one month later, as a show much closer to Terry's heart than *Shock Theatre*, his Emmy-nominated children's series *The Jobblewocky Place*, also got the hook.

Terry Turner, who had interviewed Terry Bennett back in 1958, announced in his June 8, 1962, *Chicago Daily News* article "Summer Line-up Changes" that Bennett was to be let go, along with local WBKB stars Marty Faye, TV chef Francois Pope of *Creative Cookery*, and Dale Young of the woman's show *Clock-A-Doodle Day*:

> Marty Faye, Francois Pope, Terry Bennett and Dale Young will be dropped from the WBKB line-up at the end of the month. Some will return later, in new program formats.
>
> The station will add a new woman's show in the daytime schedule, expand Jim Stewart's *Here's Geraldine* children's show and fill in with some films.... The plans also are to bring Bennett and the *Jobblewocky Place* children's show back to the air in the fall on a once-a-week basis. The series probably would be scheduled during Saturdays.

Quinlan gave a somewhat different announcement to Paul Malloy in the *Chicago Sun-Times* writer's June 12 "It's the Malloy" column. The WBKB executive explained that he was distressed over having to cancel Bennett's very popular show, and told Malloy *why* that decision had been made.

> ... "The big problem," he explained, "is that we have too many children's shows (*Clock, Here's Geraldine*, etc.) and not enough sponsors to go around. Sponsors don't get too excited over children's programs, even when they're highly rated, because youngsters don't buy anything.
>
> "We think very highly of Bennett. He has a heck of a lot of talent and he's been doing a fine job; however, he's at his very best with the toddler audience. We're going to keep him busy this summer, and I expect we can come up with a new format — possibly for the teenage crowd — in the fall."

However, no Terry Bennett–starring show aimed at teenagers ever materialized on Channel 7, and Terry never became the Chicago equivalent of Dick Clark (anyway, a niche already occupied by local celeb Jim Lounsbury).

A Wacky Last Show at WBKB

Terry Bennett's career at WBKB was still not over, as an in-house publication soon announced "Terry Bennett will return to WBKB's program line-up with an all-new show, *The Wacky World of Mr. B* on Saturday. Sept. 29."

In 1962, Terry produced, wrote and starred in the final WBKB show with which he would be involved, *The Wacky World of Mr. B*. Unlike *The Jobblewocky Place*, the new program was not on a very hectic five-day-per-week schedule, but aired just once per week — at nine o'clock on Saturday mornings. Although different from *The Jobblewocky Place*, *The Wacky World of Mr. B*. was still infused with the same brand of Terry Bennett kookiness. *Wacky World* reviews were good; one of them appeared in "Time Out," a section of the December 1962 issue of *The PTA Magazine*:

This dapper young man is a natural humorist, and we find his zany world almost as amusing as the children do. It is not a slapstick world, but one of diverting illogic, in which the only thing you can expect is that the next incident will be unexpected. Some of the jests are old, but many are new and fresh, and — the great thing — nearly all are funny. Mr. B. is a talented ventriloquist, too, and as such is ably seconded by an attractive puppet in the Charlie McCarthy tradition.

Don't watch this program if you like only jokes that make sense. Here are some samples of the wacky wit of Mr. B: "Why does Napoleon, in his pictures, always hold his hand in his pocket?" "To hold his pants up." Mr. B cures his puppet of the hiccups only to get them himself. He does a splendid burlesque of a concerto, but after he finishes, the music keeps right on playing. (An oldie, but still irresistible.) We have particularly enjoyed the clips of old movies in which there suddenly appears Mr. B's inquiring face, earnestly breaking into the conversation and of course never receiving a reply. It's a small reflection of Groucho Marx's wackiness, with none of Marx's sting; you might say it separates the boys from the men.

When *The Wacky World of Mr. B.* finally wrapped in 1963, the Bennetts decided that they had given enough of their time, talent and lives to local Chicago television. Soon they would be packing their things and leaving their Schiller Park home, heading back towards Terry's original home state of New York.

Nevertheless, working on *Shock Theatre* seems to have been a pleasant experience for him as well as the other members of the cast. As Bruce Newton told Rick Thomas in *Filmfax*:

Everyone was very close. We'd sit around in the prop room with the stage hands. It was down-to-earth fun. They'd play tricks and jokes. But as soon as the floor director said, "Going on in ten seconds," everyone was silent and there wasn't a peep. Everyone was professional.

Likewise, Joy Bennett's memories of performing on *Shock Theatre* were warm, as she told Ted Okuda and Mark Yurkiw: "We worked together as a family — the stagehands, the soundman, everybody. It was all good healthy fun."

Fun indeed, but for Terry and Joy Bennett, and also Bruce Newton, *Shock Theatre* was also past history.

14

Aftershock

Although *Shock Theatre* had ended, the careers of its various cast members — excluding, of course, Mr. Bones and the Glob — continued.

The musicians who had comprised Marvin's Deadbeats continued to work consistently, playing in studio recording session, for commercials, other television shows and live gigs.

Bruce Newton continued wearing his many hats and performing myriad duties at WBKB following his "unmasking" on *Shock Theatre*. For a while, during the late 1960s, he also served as an instructor, teaching broadcasting subjects at Columbia College in downtown Chicago.

In 1964, when Sterling "Red" Quinlan left WBKB, Newton relocated to another local station, WCIU (Channel 26), famed as Chicago's first UHF (ultra-high frequency channel. Newton, along with long-time WBKB entertainer Dick "Two Ton" Baker, was assigned to work on another children's program and also to do more promotions. As far as Newton's career was concerned, very little had changed.

While working at Channel 26, Newton met an attractive woman named Claire, who would soon become his wife. Together the Newtons would work on numerous new programs, including Don Cornelius' very long-running hit show *Soul Train*. Semi-retiring in 1976, both Newtons left WCIU to go on the road performing live puppet shows, always dressed in blacks and reds, and taking with them the original Garfield Goose puppet that, decades before, Bruce had created.

In 2006, shortly after Claire passed away, Bruce died at the age of 80 in an Aurora, Illinois, nursing home.

Ronny Born continued to work at WBKB following the cancellation of *Shock Theatre*. As he told the author:

> *Shock Theatre* was a huge success. Young people loved it. (My mother hated it, but everyone else in my family thought it was great that I was working.) The

A 2002 photograph of Bruce Newton (right) with Rick Thomas (aka TV horror host "Lazlo, Keeper of the Dead"), wearing a Frankenstein Monster mask (not the Don Post kind Newton wore on *Shock Theatre*). Newton was still making personal appearances as Shorty, wearing this new mask, around the time this picture was taken (courtesy Rick Thomas).

show was abruptly terminated in 1959 through no fault of its own. The network which owned our station put in boxing and wanted our time slot. It still enjoyed top ratings, but you didn't argue with City Hall, at least not in Chicago. We all went back to our daytime jobs and that was that.

In 1966, following his long association with WBKB and WLS, Sterling "Red" Quinlan helped found another local Chicago television station, WFLD (Channel 32), and became its first general manager. By the early 1970s, WFLD had its own program with a format inspired by *Shock Theatre*: *Screaming Yellow Theatre* starred local disc jockey Jerry G. Bishop as Svengoolie, a kind of spooky parody of a hippie. As Svengoolie, Bishop wore pasty make-up, a crepe mustache and wig, both green, and the kind of attire sometimes seen on Hollywood's Sunset Strip back in the middle 1960s. Like Marvin, Svengoolie ran horror movies and, during the commercial breaks, acted out humorous skits, sometimes while playing a guitar.

After Bishop abandoned the role, he was succeeded by another horror host, also wearing heavy make-up and performing a similar act, although without the *faux* hippie trappings. Bishop's successor was actually a young fan named Rich Koz, who adopted the role of Son of Svengoolie. Koz' Show, originally called *Son of Svengoolie*, began on WFLD in 1979. Like Marvin and his own predecessor, Svengoolie ran horror movies and performed macabre skits, some of them musical. To date of this writing, more than three decades later, the Svengoolie program is still running on Channel 32,*with Koz a popular Windy City celebrity. It is now seen in more markets than just the Chicago area.

Sterling Quinlan died in 2007 of respiratory failure at the age of 91.

A Sterling Recommendation

On July 30, 1963, before Terry Bennett and his family left for New York, Quinlan typed on American Broadcasting Company stationery the following letter of endorsement, to be read by the Bennetts' potential new employers:

To whom it concerns:
It is a distinct pleasure to give an unqualified endorsement of Terry Bennett who has worked with WBKB in Chicago for years.

Terry Bennett is indeed a triple threat man. He has done some of the outstanding kid shows ever seen in Chicago. He produces. He writes. He does an acceptable job as a staff announcer. He is a good master of ceremonies. He is a stable asset to any station's roster.

Along with his wife, Terry Bennett created several outstanding successes at WBKB, the most notable among them being *Jobble Wocky Place* [sic] and *The Wacky World of Mr. B.*

Terry has accepted each of his assignments cheerfully and with the sense of creative challenge that marks a true professional. An example of his ability to meet a creative need occurred at WBKB when he was commissioned to come up with a host character for *Shock Theater*, [sic], a package of horror films. Mr. Bennett not only came up with a marvelous, grotesque characterization, but he wrote his own material for an ensemble of musicians which mounted these films in a splendidly humorous setting. *Shock Theater* was a huge success as much because of Terry Bennett as for any other reason. Here is an extremely talented man and I recommend him without any reservations whatsoever.

S. C. Quinlan

Quinlan's missive, though flattering to his former jack-of-many trades, somehow neglected to mention that Terry was not just "commissioned" to invent a format and host character for *Shock Theatre*, but that he had originally come to Quinlan with the idea for the show, an idea that included the character of Marvin.

* CURRENTLY ON ME TV (CHANNEL 26.3)

The Bennetts Take Manhattan

Now living suburban New Rochelle, New York, Terry found new opportunities (and more of them), at least for a while, to utilize his numerous
talents. New York City, its cosmopolitan atmosphere and numerous television
stations, some of them telecasting network rather than just local programs,
might have more to offer the Bennetts than provincial WBKB. As Joy told
Rick Thomas in *Filmfax*, "When we moved back to New York, he was able
to get involved in producing, directing, and inventing those ideas that lent
themselves so well to the TV audience."

—m—

In New York, Terry went to work for local station WPIX (Channel 11).
At that station produced a *Jobblewocky*-like show called *The Chuck McCann
Show*, *The Sammy Kaye Show*, and David Susskind's *Hot Line*; developed,
wrote and budgeted numerous commercials and other programs; executive-
produced *The Clay Cole Show* (celebrated as the second show in the United
States to book the Rolling Stones), and, from 1965 to 1967, returned to performing in another *Jobblewocky*-type show, *Let's Have Fun*.

During this period of Terry's career, the Bennetts adopted a little girl,
Jill, born in May, 1965; then, the following year, Joy gave birth to a son,
Kerry.

By 1970, Terry's affection for his old Marvin character seems to have
waned to pretty much zero. Tellingly, perhaps, his professional résumé of that
year, while listing numerous credits, some of them comparatively quite trivial,
did not mention *Shock Theatre* or anyone connected with it.

The Florida Move

In 1972, the Bennett family again relocated, this time to Tampa in Joy's
home state of Florida. Once settled in their new home, Terry was hired by
local station WTOG (Channel 44) where he hosted a Saturday morning children's show that played the Our Gang comedies (re-christened "The Little
Rascals" when the shorts were released to television in the 1950s) and anchored
a news show. For the Little Rascals sponsor, Burger King, Terry created a new
character, BK Lion, that he himself played wearing a full-body costume. Like
Marvin, BK would introduce the films, do funny skits and also, as the lion's
popularity grew, make personal appearances.

On October 12, 1977, after two years suffering from a serious illness, and almost 18 years to the day after bidding farewell to his *Shock Theatre* television audience, Terry Bennett died at the too-young age of 47.

Very sadly, Joy Bennett followed Terry on December 15, 2005, dying in her sleep of natural causes. It was nearly 48 years exactly since the first *Shock Theatre* episode aired on Chicago television.

Shock Theatre's *Legacy*

Who was or is the best television horror host?

It has often been said that, when asked this question, a person generally responds by naming the character that he or she watched on their local TV channel during their childhood or teenage years. That is certainly understandable.

Naturally the present writer is partial to Marvin, as should be obvious to the reader by now. However, the author's own reasons for singling out Terry Bennett and his character go beyond personal nostalgia.

More than a half century has passed since Screen Gems' *Shock!* and *Son of Shock!* packages were first shown on local television channels, introduced by characters like Roland, Tarantula Ghoul and Marvin. And during those 50-plus years there have been many, shows, some actually called *Shock Theatre* (or *Theater*), others, though basically the same kind of show, bearing names like *Museum of Horors, Creature Features* and *Screaming Yellow Theatre*. These shows all ran some or all of the Screen Gems titles and may have run other movies as well, and they had their own hosts to introduce those films.

Well over 50 years of *Shock Theatre*–type shows! That's a very long legacy for the *Shock Theatre* kind of local-television-show format — meaning a *lot* of shows and about just as many horror hosts.

But surely not every character who ever appeared on a local channel, introducing movies like *Frankenstein* and *Dracula* and performing humorous horror-based skits, can qualify as *best*.

It is not within the scope of this book to attempt compiling a checklist of all the local programs that have, over so many years, shown old horror movies hosted by some strange or sinister master or mistress of ceremonies. Many horror hosts, like Zacherley (aka Roland) and Vampira, already mentioned, have been exceptional, achieving recognition and fame. A few other such horror hosts will be noted here.

In 1964, veteran character actor Fred Stuthman was hired by local Los Angeles television station KCOP (Channel 13) to host its popular *Jeepers Creepers Theater*. The program's original horror host, named Jeepers, had been played from 1962 to 1963 by the station's program director Bob Guy. When Guy left in 1963, his replacement was Ghoulita, a sexy though scary female

character played by actress
Lietta Harvey. Bob Burns,
who had appeared as vari-
ous monsters (including a
werewolf) on KENS'
(Channel 5) version of
Shock Theatre, airing from
San Antonio, Texas, and
who had appeared (as var-
ious horrors, including the
"Mad Mummy") with Guy
during his stint on the
show, did Harvey's fright
make-up.

Stuthman created the
new character Jeepers'
Keeper for the show and
did his own make-up. Like
Terry Bennett, Stuthman
brought his many years as
a professional stage (*e.g.,*
The Drunkard) and screen

Fred Stuthman (in 1964) applies his own make-
up for his character Jeepers' Keeper, the horror
host of *Jeepers Creepers Theatre,* a show that was
videotaped at Los Angeles local station KCOP
(Channel 13).

actor to the fore in his television role, resulting in a well-rounded characterization. Jeepers' Keeper had a female sidekick, although one not as comely as
Marvin's Dear; his was the Little Old Lady from Pasadena, in reality an inanimate skull-headed dummy. *Jeepers Creepers Theater* ran the old Universal
horror movies but also low-budget titles (*e.g., The Mad Monster, The Devil
Bat*) made by Poverty Row companies during the 1930s and 1940s.

Like Terry Bennett and Fred Stuthman, Larry Vincent was already a professional actor when he created his character Sinister Seymour in 1970 for
Fright Night, a series originating at Los Angeles television station KHJ (Channel 9). Vincent wore a black cape and wide-brimmed hat, but required no
special make-up to sell his character. Having a thin face with high cheekbones,
Vincent boasted that he resembled character actor John Carradine, which was
sufficient for his characterization.

Vincent's Seymour was cynical, sarcastic and also blatantly honest, calling
the movies he showed on his program as he saw them (he labeled most of
them, like *Attack of the Mushroom People* and *Monster from the Surf,* "turkeys"),
When Seymour got better movies, like Universal's classic *Bride of Frankenstein,*
his tone changed from mocking to reverent. Seymour became a popular Los

The author and Linda Gray with TV horror host Sinister Seymour (Larry Vincent) in the early 1970s. Vincent made numerous personal appearances as Seymour, such as hosting a theatrical screening of the 1968 horror movie *Night of the Living Dead.*

Angeles–area figure on the personal appearance circuit, showing up at movie premieres, horror and film conventions, awards ceremonies and other events.

Elvira, Mistress of the Dark, as impersonated by red-haired movie actress Cassandra Peterson, was a kind of successor to Maila Nurmi's Vampira. The beautiful and well-endowed Peterson premiered her character in 1989 on the syndicated television series *Movie Macabre.* The Elvira character, sort of an outrageous combination of vampire, witch, sex goddess and "Valley Girl," became an instant sensation. Most of the movies she showed were low-grade cheapies like *Frankenstein's Daughter* and, like Seymour, Peterson had no qualms about branding such fare accordingly. She also presented some good films, like the Vincent Price thriller *House of Wax,* which she showed on her series in its original 3D format.

Peterson's fetching appearance, with her alabaster complexion, huge black wig, and her clinging black gown with its plunging, cleavage-revealing neckline, quickly spawned a line of licensed merchandise, bookings for numerous TV and radio guest shots, countless personal appearances, movie cameos, even two feature-length motion pictures, *Elvira, Mistress of the Dark* (1989) and the (pun-intended) *Elvira's Haunted Hills* (2002). As of this writing, Cassandra Peterson is still performing, on satellite TV and elsewhere, as Elvira.

Like Terry Bennett, Fred Stuthman, Larry Vincent and Cassandra Peterson, Dick Dyszel was a professional actor when, in 1973, he created his vampire horror host Count Gore De Vol for *Creature Feature*, a show emanating from Washington, D.C. television station WDCA (Channel 20). Wearing full Dracula-style makeup and attire and speaking in a Lugosi-inspired accent, Dyszel's Count has, over the years, evolved into a kind of "grand maestro" of horror hosts.

Dick Dyszel, like so many of his contemporaries, has too often been required to run some of the less prestigious entries in horror and science fiction genres, movies like *The Astro-Zombies* and *Mars Needs Women*. But his brainchild is celebrated as one of the most enduring of all horror host characters, second in longevity only to Zacherley. Indeed, Dyszel has kept the character of Count Gore De Vol undead and active for nearly four decades. On July 11, 1998, he brought his humorous vampire creation to cyberspace, launching the first series of movies having its own horror host — called *Creature Feature*, naturally — on the World Wide Web.

Most of the earliest television horror hosts were "originals," characters not inspired by any that had gone before, because there really weren't any. Those "originals" included Drana Badour and Vampira, followed by those numbering among the "first wave" of *Shock!* film package hosts, like Roland, Gorgon and Marvin.

But many of the horror hosts that appeared in later years were derivative, fitting an image apparently perceived by some of them as traditional or even correct. Many horror hosts seem cut from the same bolt of black cloth — that is, a creepy or nerdy, usually male character, the face heavily created in pasty-white facial make-up, with black circles under the eyes, black shading or striations darkening the cheeks, black lips, a messy gray fright wig, and an old-fashioned suit with cape and top hat. Often their style of patter is also interchangeable.

Too many horror hosts, both of the past and present, have been poorly defined, if defined at all. Just *what* are the characters *supposed to be*? And *why* do they *look and talk* the way they do? Are they ghouls, vampires, zombies? If so, then the pasty faces and blackened eye sockets kind of make sense.

But some of these white-faced, dark-lipped and top-hat–wearing characters seem to be just mortal human beings — agreed, sometimes mad doctors, gravediggers or just plain storytellers, but human nonetheless. That being the case, the question arises as to *why* they wear the heavy make-up and dress like they do. Are they merely eccentrics who enjoy hiding their faces under layers of Stein's clown white and black greasepaint and decking themselves out in the styles of some earlier century?

With home video recorders, DVD burners, webcams, cable-access television, YouTube and the like readily accessible, it is relatively easy for some enterprising soul who loves both horror movies and black humor and performing to become a "horror host." The criteria seem simple enough: Just put on the make-up, slip on the outfit and start performing.

With the inexpensively available technology of today, the horror host phenomenon has proliferated. They are ubiquitous at such horror-themed events as movie premieres, parties and book, CD and DVD signings. Entire conventions have been devoted to the current breed of horror hosts, where self-styled practitioners of the craft attend *en masse*, maybe outnumbering the guests. Many of them look and sound as if they belong to the same family.

Marvin's Mystique

Four factors need to be stressed concerning Terry Bennett and the character he created and portrayed.

First, Terry's Marvin — like Roland Zacherley and Vampira — was an *original* character, not one based upon some TV horror host that had preceded him.

Second, Marvin was a *well-defined* character. Viewers knew exactly *who* Marvin was and *what* he was. He was a beatnik; and being one of that class of 1950s "non-conformists," he, like so many "beats" of the era, dressed the part. Also, Marvin was supposed to be near-sighted; hence, those thick-glass lenses.

Unlike other beatniks, however, Marvin viewed life (and death) from his own unique and extremely twisted point of view. Marvin perceived nothing wrong in perpetrating acts against Dear that, if committed by someone else, would have been deemed horrendous, not to mention against the law and warranting multiple life prison sentences and several death penalties. In that sense Marvin was a kind of "innocent" who could (and many times did) literally get away with murder. He was right and the world around him was, well, "not right," at least in his own mind — which may be one reason "Shock Absorbers" loved Marvin.

Third, Marvin was (especially without those magnifying glasses) attractive and charismatic. He was also "hip" and "cool," certainly no nerd or creep like so many other horror host characters. Except for possibly displaying some surprising table manners, especially when handling knives, and occasionally cackling maniacally, Marvin might be someone to invite home for a family dinner ... even someone to emulate. There was nothing wrong, back in the '50s, with dressing like Marvin — putting on the black turtleneck, the jacket, the shades — and going out on a date. Indeed, there *still* isn't. But how many horror host fans would relish being seen on the street or at some social gathering wearing the white make-up, cape and top hat?

Finally, the man behind Marvin's persona was not just some TV stagehand or floor manager — someone with no talent for or experience in performing — drafted into playing a character for which he or she might not be suited or have the ability to play. Terry was an extremely talented (and multitalented) professional entertainer, backed up by a solid résumé of performing before ever donning the garb and glasses of Marvin. Moreover, Terry was not only qualified to play the role of Marvin, he also possessed what was required to write the character's material.

Terry created a fully developed and credible character for Chicago's *Shock Theatre* and brought that character to life on the small TV screen. And he accomplished this *without* the need to hide his features under layers of fright make-up or put on weird, creepy or funny clothes.

Afterword
by Dick Dyszel,
"Count Gore De Vol"

It was a dark and stormy night in 1957 ... or at least dark, because it was night ... a Saturday night. My parents were asleep as I quietly crept out of my room, making my way to the 21-inch Admiral TV in the living room. Turing it on as quietly as possible, I grabbed a towel to wrap around the tuning knob. Ever so carefully I turned it, trying to minimize the "ka-thunk" made by the mechanical tuner as it went past each channel. Finally it came to rest on Channel 7, WBKB, and there in bright and shiny black and white was my weekly dose of classic horror on *Shock Theatre*, hosted by the most unlikely of hosts ... Marvin, the Near-Sighted Madman!

While the 80s' had their "punk" scene and the 60s' had the "hippie" scene, the 50s' alternative social style was "the beat" scene, epitomized by the beatnik. Wearing black, including the ever present shades and/or thick-rimmed glasses, the beatniks hung out at coffee houses, digging on the latest poetry ... at least that's the way I remember it. But on weekends, Marvin brought the "beat" sensibility to the world of classic Universal horror films, exposing young minds like mine to all sorts of alternative possibilities.

Marvin, played by ventriloquist Terry Bennett, was not alone. His side-kick and the butt of most of his jokes was Dear, his real-life wife, Joy Bennett. She was blond, wore tight clothes and had a couple of points of her own ... riding way up high. However, we had no idea what she looked like because she always had her face away from the camera or covered ... the ultimate tease.

Marvin also had his own band, the Deadbeats, that performed live during the breaks in the movie. They also added Orville, a hunchback character, and Shorty, a giant monster wearing a Frankenstein mask! Horror classics, beatniks, offbeat humor and music ... what more could a ten-year-old want late on a Saturday night?

To be honest, I don't specifically remember any of the bits from the show.

Count Gore De Vol (Dick Dyszel).

I do remember they were both funny and silly and were a perfect match for my pre-adolescent taste. I know that I watched regularly and that eventually my parents actually allowed me to stay up and watch without all the sneaking around.

The show lasted for only two years. In spite of tremendous popularity and a petition campaign, it was cancelled to make way for boxing! It was during the last show that we finally got to see the lovely face of Dear. The truly sad thing is that there seems to be only one video clip of the show and that was actually shot during a rehearsal session. *http://www.youtube.com/watch?v= GsEALyn2qyM*

The audio for the final show, courtesy of Terry Tiz, has been captured and a slide show of stills have been added here: *http://www.youtube.com/watch ?v=lOxZbh2rk7I&NR=1*

Terry Bennett had a full career as an entertainer. You can learn about it at: *http://www.chicagotelevision.com/bennett.htm*

You'll also find a huge number of stories and pictures at: *http://monsterkidclassichorrorforum.yuku.com/topic/24138/t/Chicago-s-legendary-Marvin-on-Shock-Theatre.html*

Fast forwarding to 1970, I found myself in the WDXR-TV conference room in Paducah, Kentucky, helping the general manager pick from a package of filmed program openings. After too many hours of watching, I blurted out, "What we need is a hosted horror movie!"

He slowly turned to me and replied, "You're hired!"

Now the perfect conclusion to this story would have been a revival of *Shock Theatre* with a Marvin clone. But life's never perfect. The "beat" movement was dead. I owned a tux and a cape, but no black turtleneck. So, I was destined to develop a vampire character who would be known to the world as Count Gore De Vol! A character that would be the preeminent horror host of Washington, DC on WDCA's Creature *Feature* and then become the first horror host of the Internet (at www.countgore.com).

But this no way diminishes the uniqueness of Marvin and *Shock Theatre* or its impact on my life. In the 40 years that I've been hosting horror movies and researching other horror hosts, there has never been another Marvin! Terry Bennett created a unique horror host. He was perfect for his time and his market and as such, made a profound impact on his audience.

If I hadn't watched and enjoyed the two years of *Shock Theatre*, I would not have uttered those fateful words that started my career as a TV and now Internet horror host. When struggling to figure out what a horror host was and what he did, I was able to fall back on my memories of Marvin. Yes, if you're going to steal, steal from the best ... and I most certainly did!

Life is full of opportunities and regrets. I was fortunate to have the opportunity to watch *Shock Theatre*. I regret I didn't have the opportunity to meet and get to know Terry and Joy Bennett. I'm happy to have had the opportunity to become a fellow horror host, but I regret that the genius that started me down that path is limited to still pictures, a bit of audio and one short video clip. This past March, I had the opportunity to witness the induction of Terry Bennett into the Horror Host Hall of Fame.

Washington, D.C.

2012

Appendix I.
Marvin's "Cartoon" Line-Up

Following is a list of all the motion pictures run by Marvin (and, in a few instances, Basil), played by Terry Bennett, on *Shock Theatre.*

The movies (frequently referred to by Marvin as "cartoons") are listed in the order, with dates, in which they were run. Unless otherwise stated, each show began at 10:00 PM. The list is accurate, as can best be determined, based upon researching back issues of *TV Guide,* local television newspaper and guide book schedules, and also the author's memory.

The list *only* cites the films that were shown while Bennett was involved with the program. Following Terry and Joy Bennett's departure, a program called *Shock Theatre* aired from October 23 through much of 1960, still showing the *Shock!* and *Son of Shock!* movies; but those episodes are *not* included on this list.

1957
December 7 —*Frankenstein*
December 14 — *The Wolf Man*
December 21—*Night Monster*
December 28 — *The Mummy*

1958
January 4 —*Murders in the Rue
      Morgue*
January 11—*Dracula*
January 18 — *WereWolf of London*
January 25 — *The Spider Woman
      Strikes Back*
February 1— *The Invisible Man*

February 8 — *The Black Cat*
February 15 — *The Mummy's Hand*
February 22 —*Secret of the Blue Room*
March 1—*Dracula's Daughter*
March 8 — *The Invisible Ray*
March 15 —*Man Made Monster*
March 22 —*Dr. Renault's Secret*
March 29 — *The Mad Doctor of
      Market Street*
April 5 — *Cry of the Werewolf*
April 12 —*Son of Frankenstein*
April 19 — *The Soul of a Monster*
April 26 — *The Mad Ghoul*
May 3 —*Calling Dr. Death*

181

May 10 — *The Invisible Man Returns*

May 17 — *Dead Man's Eyes*

May 31 — *The Frozen Ghost*

May 24 — *The Mummy's Tomb*

June 7 — *Son of Dracula*

June 14 — *The Cat Creeps*

June 21 — *House Of Horrors*

June 28 — *Pillow Of Death*

July 5 — *Mystery of Edwin Drood*

July 12 — *The Return of the Vampire*

July 19 — *The Son of Kong*

July 26 — *Weird Woman*

August 2 — *Frankenstein Meets the Wolf Man*

August 9 — *The Body Snatcher*

August 16 — *The Strange Case of Doctor RX*

August 23 — *The Raven*

August 30 — *She-Wolf of London*

September 6 — *The Mummy's Ghost*

September 13 — *The Brighton Strangler*

September 20 — *Frankenstein*

September 27 — *The Undying Monster*

October 4 — *I Walked with a Zombie*

October 11 — *Bride of the Monster* [*Shocktail Party* begins]

October 18 — *The Wolf Man*

October 25 — *Night of Terror*

November 1 — *The Face Behind the Mask*

November 8 — *Bride of Frankenstein*

November 15 — *Night Monster*

November 22 — *The Black Room*

November 29 — *Island of Doomed Men*

December 6 — *The Invisible Man's Revenge*

December 13 — *The Mummy*

December 20 — *The Man They Could Not Hang*

December 27 — *Murders in the Rue Morgue*

1959

January 3 — *Dracula*

January 10 — "The Ape Woman" [*The Jungle Captive*]

January 17 — *Son of Frankenstein*

January 24 — *Before I Hang*

January 31 — *Werewolf of London*

February 7 — *House of Dracula*

February 14 — *The Spider Woman Strikes Back*

February 21 — *The Mummy's Hand*

February 28 — *The Invisible Man*

March 7 — *The Ghost of Frankenstein*

March 14 — *Dr. Renault's Secret*

March 21 — *The Black Cat* [starts at 11:00]

March 28 — *Dracula's Daughter*

April 4 — *Man Made Monster*

April 11 — *The Mummy's Curse*

April 18 — *The Invisible Ray*

April 25 — *The Human Monster*

May 2 — *Black Friday*

May 9 — *The Mad Ghoul*

May 16 — *Frankenstein Meets The Wolf Man*

May 23 — *Behind The Mask*

May 30 — *Cry of the Werewolf*

June 6 — "Return of the Ape Woman" [*Captive Wild Woman*]

June 13 — *The Invisible Man Returns*

June 20 — *The Mummy's Tomb*

June 27 — *Son of Dracula*

July 4 — *The Mad Doctor of Market Street*

July 11—*House of Frankenstein*

July 18 — *The Soul of a Monster*

July 25 —*House of Horrors*

August 1—*The Devil Commands*

August 8 — *The Cat Creeps*

August 15 — *The Man Who Lived Twice*

August 22—*Weird Woman* [starts at 11:30]

August 29 — *The Raven* [starts at 11:30]

September 5 —pre-empted by Pan-American basketball and professional football

September 12 —*Hangover Square* [starts at 11:30]

September 19 — *The Undying Monster* [starts at 11:30]

September 26 — *The Man with Nine Lives* [starts at 11:30]

October 3 — *The Strange Case of Doctor. Rx* [starts at midnight]

October 10—*She-Wolf of London* [back to 10:00]

October 17 —*Bride of the Monster*

Appendix II.
Terry Bennett Résumé

Terry Bennett, 11 Edna Place, New Rochelle, N.Y. (914) 235-1915

Résumé

Television and advertising executive with production and successful experience and a successful track record of creating and administering successful broadcast and advertising programs on schedule that work and budgets that cut costs.

Experience

Broadcast

Teleradio Corp. (1967–79) Executive radio/TV producer. Supervised all Media selection and broadcast activities for Castro Convertibles. Wrote and Produced commercials used in 11 major markets. During the time I was responsible for Castro campaigns, business rose 67 percent.

WPIX, Ch, 11 NYC (1962–67) Executive producer. Producer on David Susskind's *Hot Line, Let's Have Fun,* the *Clay Cole Shows,* the *Chuck McCann Shows,* the *Sammy Kaye Show.* In addition to program development and concepts, my responsibilities included script and budget supervision as well as supervision over Videotape production of both programs and commercials.

ABC-TV, WBKB-TV, Chi. (1954–1962) Over an 8 year span, I was a writer, producer, on-air promotion director, and program development coordinator. I was nominated for three Emmy Awards, and received national commendation for programming excellence. I created the on-air logos for the ABC network and did the on-air promotion for such network shows as *Maverick* and *Tennessee Ernie Ford.* Also involved in creative production of commercials for Midas Mufflers, Delco batteries, Turtle Wax, Rival Dog Food, and Kellogg Cereals.

184

Special Assignments. I have handled special projects (production and promotion) for WGN, WBBM-TV, and WMAQ-TV (all Chicago), WTVJ (Miami), WCBS-TV (N.Y.) and radio stations WLS (Chicago) and WFAS (New York)

Advertising

Chock Full O'Nuts (1968) Vice President — Advertising. Responsible for TV film commercials — creation, production and media selection.

Castro Convertibles (1967–70) Advertising Manager. In addition to radio and TV commercials, I was responsible for all print advertising, I created copy and layouts and personally made media buys in 11 markets.

Lazar-Bennett, Inc. (1956–59) Creative supervisor for Chicago agency. Originated advertising concepts and supervised production (all media) for a variety of clients including Ronco Construction, McDonald's (pre-franchise) and Community Discount stores.

Polk Bros. (1952–54) Writer and Media supervisor for midwest's largest carpeting, furniture and appliance retail chain.

Personal Data

Age 37, married, three children, veteran, excellent health, Roosevelt University/B.A. English (Nights)

Bibliography

Ackerman, Forrest J. "TerrorVision." *Famous Monsters of Filmland*, 2, 1958.
Benton, Mike. *The Illustrated History of Horror Comics*. Dallas: Taylor, 1991.
Burns, Bob, and John Michlig. *It Came from Bob's Basement*. San Francisco: Chronicle Books, 2000.
Buxton, Frank, and Bill Owen. *The Big Broadcast, 1920–1950*. New York: Viking, 1972.
Gibson, Walter B. *The Shadow Scrapbook*. New York and London: Harcourt Brace Jovanovich, 1979.
Martin, Richard A. *Mummies*. Popular Series, Anthropology, No. 36. Chicago: Field Museum of Natural History, 1940.
"Night Harbingers of Horror," *Life*, May 26, 1958.
Okuda, Ted, and Mark Yurkiw. *Chicago TV Horror Movie Shows: From Shock Theatre to Svengoolie*. Chicago: Lake Claremont Press, 2007.
Thomas, Rick. "Terry Bennett (a.k.a. 'Marvin') of Chicago's Shock Theater," *Filmfax*, 104, October-December, 2004.
Tucker, Ernest. "A Real Cool Ghoul!" *Pictorial Living*, February 16, 1959.
Warren, Bill. *Keep Watching the Skies! The 21st Century Edition*. Jefferson, NC: McFarland, 2010.
Watson, Elena M. *Television Horror Movie Hosts*. Jefferson, NC: McFarland, 1991.
Wertham, Frederick, M.D. *Seduction of the Innocent*. New York and Toronto: Rinehart & Company, 1953.
"What a Revoltin' Development!" *TV Guide*, March 29, 1958, pp. 17–19.
Willis, Donald C. *Horror and Science Fiction Films: A Checklist*. Metuchen, NJ: Scarecrow, 1972.

Index

Page numbers in **bold italics** indicate illustrations or their captions.

187